Meredith Books
1716 Locust Street
Des Moines, Iowa 50309–3023
meredithbooks.com

Printed in the United States of America.

First Edition.
Library of Congress Control Number: 2006938730
ISBN: 978-0-696-23396-8

Cover and Food Photography: Robert Jacobs
Cars courtesy of Geoff Albert, Classic Tours Classic Car Service, Savannah, GA

The recipes that appear in this book were inspired by the travels of the Deen Brothers
to the restaurants and family businesses featured herein. The recipes are the creation
of Jamie and Bobby Deen and were not contributed by the featured establishments.

The Deen Bros. Cookbook

By Jamie and Bobby Deen
and Melissa Clark

Meredith® Books
Des Moines, Iowa

For my heart and soul…
Brooke and Jack

— Jamie

For you, Mom. Thanks for making all things possible.

— Bobby

CONTENTS

THE SOUTH

Conch Republic Seafood Company	12
Henrietta's	16
Blond Giraffe	22
Tennessee T-Cakes	28
Lynchburg Cake & Candy Company	34
Neely's Bar-B-Que Restaurant	38
Butters Brownies	44
Royers Round Top Cafe	48
The County Line	54

THE MIDWEST

Beechwood Cheese Company	112
Bendtsen's Bakery	116
Sprecher Brewing Company	120
Lou Malnati's Pizzeria	124
Kim & Scott's Gourmet Pretzels	128
Solomon's Gourmet Cookies	132
Swiss Meats	138
Volpi Italian Foods	142
The Blue Owl	148

THE WEST

Flagstaff House Restaurant	62
Wen Chocolates	68
The Boulder Dushanbe Teahouse	72
Sweetie Pies	78
Marini's Candies	84
Phil's Fish Market	88
Pike Place Fish Market	92
Alaska Silk Pie	98
Macrina Bakery and Cafe	104

THE EAST

Mike's Deli	156
Veniero's	162
Landi's Pork Store	166
David Burke & Donatella	170
Artopolis	174
Zozo's	180
Morrison's Maine Course	186
Eminger Berries	190
Wicked Whoopies	194
Mom's Apple Pie Company	198
Market Inn Restaurant	204
Sticky Fingers Bakery	210

RECIPE INDEX	214
RESOURCES	222

FOREWORD FROM "MAMA," PAULA DEEN

I can honestly say that my most rewarding, yet challenging, role in life has been that of a mom. I have been blessed with two beautiful young men both in looks and in spirit. Starting out as a parent, you can only hope that you are instilling all of the right things. I tried to teach them the importance of being caring, considerate, respectful, and trustworthy. I reminded them daily that family is the most important thing and that laughter is a cure for almost anything. Self-confidence comes from within, and you can do anything you want in life if you are willing to work hard. How in the world would I have ever known that they actually listened to me? That two boys who were adorable toddlers, hard-headed as teens would grow into such wonderful kind human beings.

As I watch my boys travel throughout the country doing their show, I realize the unique qualities they possess as individuals. Bobby is the most like me in many ways. He has the hardest time saying no. I believe it actually hurts his heart to disappoint anyone he cares about. Jamie is my strong one. He stands up for what he believes in no matter the consequences. He has always been my knight in shining armor. Protecting our family is of the utmost importance. Together there is nothing they cannot do. When young boys should be headed off to college, Bobby and Jamie were helping me keep our family together. When their mother decided to open a restaurant, they were right there bussing tables and taking orders. I always encouraged them to dream big. In our wildest dreams, we could not have imagined the path that has led us to where we are today.

It fills my heart like nothing else to see them so rich with respect for others' kindness and honesty. We have been very blessed as a family, and that is why I am so proud of this book. Jamie and Bobby have searched our great country to identify others like us who are living the American dream. The recipes in this book are inspired by their travels and the people they have met along the way who are keeping traditions alive.

It is every mother's goal to give her children wings to soar. And as their wings expand it makes a proud mother's heart soar. I am so honored that they have asked me to write this introduction. Thank you, Jamie and Bobby, for taking us along on this beautiful tour of our country.

Boys, I'm so proud of y'all!!
I love you both,

Mama

Pictured from left: Bobby, Paula, and Jamie

Jamie

INTRODUCTION TO JAMIE AND BOBBY

We never planned for things to go like they have—we didn't have time to sit around and plan! It all started so small, we never could have foreseen the blessings that would come our way.

In the summer of 1989 when I [Jamie] was working in food services in Yellowstone National Park and my brother, Bobby, had a job at Circuit City, Mama called me from Savannah with an idea. "Come home," she said, and many hours on a bus later, the three of us were making sandwiches for a new start-up business that Mama called The Bag Lady. We had no storefront, no training—just our home kitchen, Mama (who knew how to cook), and us boys helping her.

We carried coolers around town to offices, asking, "Y'all want lunch?" At first folks weren't interested, but Mama knew if we showed up at the same time every day we would eventually wear them down. She was right: Once they tasted the food, business began to pick up. As we grew, we stuck to what we knew—always have, always will. We sold light salads, sandwiches, desserts, and eventually grilled chicken salads and hot meals such as chicken pot pie. Simple, satisfying Southern food, just like we love.

At the time, Bobby and I thought The Bag Lady might be a phase Mama was going through, like when she had tried being a bank teller and a

real estate agent. But business got going and not one of us had time to stop to think about what to do next. On the fly we had shirts printed, we got a delivery car, and since every day we earned enough to buy supplies for the next day, we kept at it. Before long we had a restaurant—in the Best Western. Breakfast, lunch, and dinner, seven days a week, we watched Mama work 18-hour days and we began to wonder what the point was. But then we added a Southern brunch buffet, word got out about our place, and locals started coming for the kind of home cooking they didn't have time to make for themselves: fried chicken, collards, corn bread … In a few years we were doing the buffet every day, and there were lines out the door—all of those folks waiting to taste the same cooking we had been eating at home every night of our lives!

After we were in the Best Western for five years, a developer offered us a lease on a property, so we moved across town and opened our own restaurant, The Lady & Sons.

Some loyal customers had followed us, and folks came to The Lady & Sons for lunch, but dinner business was slower than molasses. We watched lines form outside the four-star restaurants on either side of us, but not many downtown diners knew who we were. We didn't

Bobby

"Thanks to Mama, we've learned how far hard work can take us and we can't wait to see where we get to next!"

really know either; we were "Hey, how ya doin'?" guys on a "Good evening, madam" street. We wondered: Should we class up the menu, add white tablecloths, and try to compete with those other places? We tried bringing in live music but continued to offer the same foods, including fried chicken and macaroni and cheese. Mama's mantra was always "Keep it simple." We figured all we could do was offer our best food and service at a fair price and wait and see. At the restaurant I worked in the kitchen while Bobby welcomed guests and chatted with customers. We could both feel it happening: The place was filling up. Mama started working on her cookbook, we were running the restaurant, and the media began to catch on to us.

As Mama's book took off and she started appearing on the QVC shopping channel, we got busier. But we stuck with the same approach we had always used, even as we moved to a bigger space and started to deal with real crowds—lines of people who had seen Mama on television, knew about her books, and wanted to meet us. Customer service, getting to talk with the folks who make our business a success, has always been our main focus. If I was busy cooking and someone wanted to meet the brothers, well, down went the pots and pans, off went the dirty

chef's coat, and out I'd come with a smile. It was busy, but hey, we owed it all to our customers, and as Mama always says, "We don't turn anything down but our collar."

We know how hard it was to get where we are and we know how many other struggling cooks and bakers are out there trying to make a go of it. They make America such a delicious place to live. So when we had the opportunity to do our own Food Network series, we wanted to showcase local, independent businesses. Bobby and I had a great time traveling to some of America's prettiest places, meeting wonderful people, and eating amazing food. We hope that we've helped the folks we visited, giving them the kind of exposure that will help them succeed.

This book has been a dream of ours, a way of sharing our travels and bringing them back home to the kitchen, inspired by the local flavors and the amazing energy of the people we've met along the way. For us, cooking and sharing are just natural, and we're so glad to have the opportunity to share the recipes in this book. We hope the food and the stories will inspire you.

HENRIETTA'S
THE ORIGINAL™
KEY WEST
COCONUT
STRIPS

INGREDIENTS: FLOUR, EGGS, MILK, SUGAR, SHREDDED COCONUT, VEGETABLE SHORTENING, SALT, YEAST,

The South

FLORIDA

Key West, with its gorgeous marinas and beaches, is at the end of the highway at the southernmost tip of the continental United States. Looking out at the pretty sailboats against a deep blue sky, we realized that this special place has all the makings for a perfect day. Bright with tropical ingredients such as key lime, mango, and coconut, the fresh, light cooking of the area is based on just-caught fish. Healthy and full of flavor, this is the kind of food we could easily get used to. As we watched the sun set over the water, we realized Key West has the makings for a lot of perfect days.

TENNESSEE

From Memphis to Nashville, Chattanooga to Knoxville, Tennessee is our kind of state. You have college and pro football, kickin' barbecue, great music, green pastures, honky-tonks, and if you two-step over to Lynchburg, Jack Daniel's whiskey (the county is dry, so step on back before you take a sip!). Not to mention that Tennessee is the home of Elvis, the Grand Ole Opry, the mighty Mississippi, and gorgeous, long-backed Tennessee walking horses. Tennessee is known to have its share of home cookin', sweet tea, and Southern hospitality. So we came hungry. And thirsty.

TEXAS

We had heard that everything is bigger in Texas, so we came expecting big food and even bigger personalities. Austin did not disappoint. A little bit country, a little bit rock 'n' roll, Austin is an unusual city. Surrounded by rolling green hills and three lovely lakes, Austin gets 300 days of sunshine per year. It calls itself the live music capital of the world, so you have to get up early and stay out late to enjoy everything offered. And the place seems to attract quirky characters, so in addition to lip-smacking Texas barbecue, you can expect, well, just about anything.

CONCH REPUBLIC
SEAFOOD COMPANY
KEY WEST, FLORIDA

When you're surrounded by water, you get hungry for fish, and Conch Republic Seafood Company is the spot to satisfy your cravings. A classic seafood restaurant in the marina, Conch Republic Seafood Company sends out its own boats and brings in most of the fish served in Key West. As they like to say, "We pick the best and sell the rest." We arrived at the restaurant at the same time as the most beautiful black grouper we'd ever seen, fresh off the boat. Grouper is one of Bobby's all-time favorites, so we knew we'd have to check out the Company's grouper with juju sauce.

We helped fillet and pan-cook the fish, then discovered some of the amazing sauces these guys make. Juju is an old recipe (or so the story goes) that originated with a pirate who spilled some rum in the sauce for his dinner. It is like a Caribbean version of our favorite barbecue sauces, based on sweet onions, mustard, honey, red wine vinegar, cayenne, cloves, cumin, and a spoonful of brown sugar. The Key West kick comes from a combo of coconut rum, mango, orange, and passion fruit. It's light and low-fat, and boy is it tangy!

The juju was absolutely delicious but didn't overwhelm the fish, which was served on a helping of Caribbean callaloo, which resembles spinach. On that ocean-fresh grouper, the juju was like a tropical vacation, like Key West on a plate.

Sauteed Spinach with Sweet Vidalia Onion

A favorite dish served at Conch Republic Seafood Company features callaloo (KAL-lah-loo), an edible green leaf widely used throughout the Caribbean. Our tasty version uses spinach, which is available everywhere.

2   tablespoons olive oil
1   Vidalia onion, thinly sliced
3   6-ounce bags prewashed
     baby spinach
     Salt and freshly ground
        black pepper

1. In a large saute pan, heat oil over medium heat. Add the onion and cook for 5 to 7 minutes or until translucent, stirring occasionally. Add the spinach; cook for 2 to 3 minutes or until wilted. Season to taste with salt and pepper.

makes 6 servings

Zesty Grilled Grouper >

We love to grill our fish outdoors. The combo of orange juice, ginger, and hot sauce, inspired by the sunny flavors of Florida, makes this recipe sing. Grouper is a great fish for grilling. Red snapper or halibut will work too.

6	6-ounce grouper fillets
6	tablespoons olive oil plus additional for brushing
1	teaspoon grated orange zest
6	tablespoons freshly squeezed orange juice
1	tablespoon grated fresh gingerroot
1	teaspoon hot sauce or to taste
1	teaspoon salt
	Freshly ground black pepper

1. Place the fish in a large nonmetal dish. Whisk together the 6 tablespoons oil, the orange zest, orange juice, gingerroot, hot sauce, salt, and pepper to taste; pour over the fish. Cover and marinate in the refrigerator for 30 to 60 minutes.

2. Meanwhile, prepare grill. Brush the fish with additional oil. Grill until fish just flakes when tested with a fork, about 5 minutes per side for each inch of thickness.

makes 6 servings

Mango Coconut Rice >

We came home from the Florida Keys putting coconut milk in everything we could think of. This pilaf is one of our best coconut recipes—the mango in it is a sweet-tart surprise.

1	tablespoon olive oil
1½	cups long grain rice
1	14-ounce can unsweetened coconut milk
⅔	cup water
1	teaspoon salt
1	large ripe mango, peeled and cubed

1. In a large saucepan, heat the oil over medium-high heat. Add the rice and stir to coat with the oil. Add the coconut milk, water, and salt; bring to a boil. Stir in the mango. Cover, reduce heat to low, and simmer about 20 minutes or until the liquid is absorbed.

2. Remove the rice from the heat and fluff it with a fork. Place a clean, dry dish towel over the pan, cover with the lid, and let steam for 5 minutes before serving.

makes 6 servings

HENRIETTA'S ™
THE ORIGINAL
KEY WEST
CONCH
ROLL ®

YUM

INGREDIENTS: FLOUR, EGGS, MILK,
SUGAR, VEGETABLE OIL, SALT, YEAST.

HENRIETTA'S
KEY WEST, FLORIDA

Before moving to Key West, Henrietta Relaford McIntosh Weaver was born and raised in Georgia, and her people are from Georgia. She has one of the warmest, sunniest dispositions imaginable. Her motto is "Food so good, you'll think we stole your mama!" and it turns out she is a real fan of our mama. Mama's story was an inspiration to her when Henrietta's Art of Baking was getting started in 1999. And this place is run on inspiration.

One of her most inspired (and popular) desserts is a crunchy, golden brown strip of coconut goodness. One customer used to buy a lot of Henrietta's coconut breads, and when Henrietta asked her how she got through those breads so fast, the lady explained that she was just addicted to the sweet, crackly topping—she didn't bother eating the whole bread.

Henrietta set out to create a dessert that would be just like that crunchy top, and the coconut strip was born. Watching her make her yeast dough, sprinkling in flour until it's just right, then rolling it real thin, we could see that she's a "pinch and dash" kind of cook. Henrietta's son, Don, helped things along by inventing a roller that cuts the dough into perfect strips. A sticky coating of boiled coconut is then spread on top and the strips are baked. They're ready to eat as soon as they're crisp and golden. Or you can get them dipped in chocolate or flavored with key lime—or both—which adds a gorgeous finish. Now that's inspired!

Southern-Style Coconut Cake

Making a big, fluffy white coconut cake takes us right back to our mama's kitchen. We start this recipe with a box of cake mix so you have more time for making the filling and frosting.

CAKE:

1	18¼-ounce package vanilla cake mix
1⅓	cups milk

COCONUT FILLING:

1	cup heavy cream
2	cups sour cream
2	cups confectioners' (powdered) sugar
1	teaspoon vanilla
3	cups shredded sweetened coconut

7-MINUTE FROSTING:

1½	cups granulated sugar
2	egg whites
⅓	cup cold water
2	teaspoons light corn syrup
	Pinch salt
1	teaspoon vanilla

Shredded fresh coconut, toasted, for decorating (about ½ cup)

1. Preheat oven to 350°F. Prepare the cake mix according to package directions, substituting the milk for water. Divide cake batter among three greased 9-inch round cake pans. Bake for 20 to 25 minutes or until golden. Let cool in pans for 10 minutes. Remove cakes from pans; cool completely on a wire rack.

2. While the cakes cool, prepare the filling. Whip the heavy cream until stiff peaks form (tips stand straight). Fold in the sour cream, then gradually fold in the confectioners' sugar. Stir in the vanilla. Fold in the sweetened coconut.

3. Using a serrated knife, split each cake in half horizontally. Spread the filling over the layers, stacking all the layers. Place the cake in an airtight container or cover tightly with plastic wrap. Refrigerate overnight or up to three days before frosting.

4. When you are ready to frost the cake, make the frosting. In the top of a double boiler or in a metal bowl, combine the granulated sugar, egg whites, water, corn syrup, and salt; beat for 1 minute with an electric hand mixer. Place the pot or bowl over (not in) a pot of boiling water. Cook, beating constantly with mixer, about 7 minutes or until the frosting becomes fluffy and stiff peaks form (tips stand straight). Remove the pot from the boiling water. Add the vanilla; continue beating for 1 to 2 minutes more or until barely warm. Frost the top and sides of the cake. Sprinkle the cake with additional coconut.

makes 12 to 16 servings

Coconut Fried Shrimp

In addition to her coconut strips, Henrietta makes a key lime-orange marmalade that is out-of-this-world good. We realized all those flavors would be great with seafood, and this recipe was born.

Vegetable oil for frying
½ cup all-purpose flour
1 teaspoon salt
½ teaspoon baking powder
⅔ cup water
2 cups shredded sweetened coconut
½ cup bread crumbs
1 pound medium or large shrimp,
    peeled and deveined

DIPPING SAUCE:
½ cup orange marmalade
4 teaspoons rice vinegar
½ teaspoon crushed red
    pepper flakes

1. In a large, heavy pot, heat 2 inches of the oil to 360°F.

2. Meanwhile, in a large bowl, whisk together the flour, salt, and baking powder. Add the water and whisk until smooth. Let the batter stand for 15 minutes.

3. In a wide, shallow bowl, toss the coconut and bread crumbs together.

4. Put the shrimp into the batter. One by one, remove the shrimp and dredge in the coconut mixture, pressing to help the coconut adhere. Fry the shrimp in batches in the hot oil for 1½ to 2 minutes or until brown. Use a slotted spoon to transfer the shrimp to a baking sheet lined with paper towels.

5. In a small, nonplastic, microwave-safe bowl, stir together the dipping sauce ingredients. Microwave on high (100% power) about 45 seconds or until bubbly. Stir and serve with the shrimp.

makes 6 appetizer servings

"Crispy shrimp in a zesty dip, what's not to love."— BOBBY

BLOND GIRAFFE
KEY WEST, FLORIDA

What's more refreshing on a hot day than a creamy, tangy piece of key lime pie? Why, a frozen slice of that pie, dipped in chocolate and complete with a handle, of course! Key limes are pale green, walnut-size limes with a strong, tart taste. They were brought to the United States from Spain 400 years ago and have become a major part of the local flavor in Key West. Still, it took a couple of Brazilians to improve on key lime pie.

Tania Beguinati and her husband, Roberto Madeira, opened Blond Giraffe in Key West in 1999. Soon after, they started winning awards for Tania's grandmother's key lime pie recipe. They expanded, opening six bakeries and a big, gleaming factory where folks can watch as the key lime magic is made. The pie features a rich cookie dough crust with some key lime zest tossed in for extra kick, a tart custard filling, and a rich, billowy meringue.

Lucky for us, Tania and Roberto didn't stop there. As soon as they heard about a place in New York that sold cheesecake on a stick, they began freezing those pies, slicing them, inserting a stick, then dipping that "pie on a stick" in chocolate. The couple is opening another location this year—after all, when you come up with something this stupendous, it would be a shame to keep it to yourself!

Key Lime Pie with Meringue Topping

This recipe is like our favorite lemon meringue pie but with the extra-tart taste of lime in it. It comes together pretty quickly and makes a refreshing dessert for a tropics-inspired meal.

FILLING:

5	large egg yolks
1	14-ounce can sweetened condensed milk
2	teaspoons grated lime zest
½	cup freshly squeezed lime juice
½	cup heavy cream
1	prepared 9-inch graham cracker crust

MERINGUE:

4	egg whites
6	tablespoons sugar
½	teaspoon cornstarch
	Pinch salt

1. Preheat the oven to 325°F. In a medium bowl, whisk together the egg yolks and condensed milk. Stir in the lime zest, lime juice, and cream. Pour the filling into the crust and bake about 20 minutes or until firm. Remove pie from oven. Increase the oven temperature to 350°F.

2. Meanwhile, in a medium bowl, beat the egg whites until soft peaks form (tips curl). In a second bowl, stir together the sugar, cornstarch, and salt. Add the sugar mixture, a little at a time, to the egg whites, beating between additions. Continue to beat until the sugar dissolves. Spoon the meringue over the hot pie filling. Bake for 10 to 12 minutes more or until the meringue is golden. Serve pie warm or at room temperature.

makes 8 servings

< Lime-Marinated Chicken Wings with Avocado Dip

*We love wings with a frosty mug of beer. Start these
a day ahead so they have a real tangy lime and chile flavor.*

MARINADE:

1½	limes
½	cup fresh cilantro leaves
¼	cup vegetable oil
2	tablespoons honey
1	to 2 jalapeño peppers, trimmed and sliced
2	teaspoons tomato paste
4	cloves garlic, chopped
	Pinch salt
3	pounds chicken wings, rinsed and patted dry
	Salt and freshly ground black pepper
	Avocado Dip (recipe at right)

1. For marinade, finely grate the zest and squeeze the juice from limes. In a blender, combine zest and juice with remaining marinade ingredients; puree until smooth. Pour marinade over the chicken and toss to coat. Cover with plastic wrap; refrigerate overnight.

2. Preheat broiler. Arrange chicken on a baking sheet. Season with salt and pepper. Broil at least 6 inches from the heat for 4 to 5 minutes per side or until chicken is crispy on the outside and cooked through. Serve with Avocado Dip.

makes 6 to 8 servings

avocado dip:

Peel and pit 1 avocado; cut into chunks. Place avocado in a medium bowl; mash. Fold in 3 tablespoons chopped fresh cilantro leaves; 1½ teaspoons lime juice; 1 clove garlic, minced; ¼ teaspoon salt; and freshly ground black pepper to taste.

Grilled Salmon with Key Lime Butter

*Once we discovered key limes, we couldn't resist using them
in a butter to flavor a rich, smoky piece of grilled salmon.*

5	tablespoons unsalted butter
2	tablespoons key lime juice
	Salt and freshly ground black pepper
4	6-ounce salmon fillets

1. Prepare grill; lightly oil grill grate. In a small saucepan, melt butter. Add lime juice, salt, and pepper. Remove from heat. Brush half of lime butter over salmon. Grill salmon for 2 to 3 minutes per side for medium rare. Drizzle remaining lime butter over salmon before serving.

makes 4 servings

TENNESSEE T-CAKES
NASHVILLE, TENNESSEE

As soon as Jamie's wife, Brooke, heard we were headed to Tennessee, she told us about Tennessee T-Cakes, which Oprah voted one of the four best cakes in the country. These little cakes are dynamite! Frances Barkley has been cooking up batches of her T-Cakes from an old Southern recipe for years. She used to give them away as gifts, and everyone came back for more, so Frances' family encouraged her to go into business. In 1991 she started in an industrial kitchen in the historic Nashville warehouse district, where her son and daughter help out.

We saw why she needs help. (When Bobby tried scooping the batter into tiny muffin tins, he got it everywhere.) It's a simple batter—flour, butter, sugar, eggs, and vanilla—and after the plain little cakes cool, they're sprinkled with powdered sugar. Take a bite and you're in for a sweet surprise. Frances says everyone tastes something different, from nuts to ginger to bourbon to cinnamon, and it's true. First they reminded us of a gooey, chewy brownie, then gingerbread. Simply amazing!

Before we left, Frances unveiled her newest product, Tennessee Brittle, inspired by the crackly bits from the T-Cakes that fall onto the cookie sheet. The tasty brittle is made from baking that batter in a thin sheet.

Lemony Honey-Almond Tea Cakes

Our version of T-Cakes uses honey, lemon, and almonds baked into scrumptious little morsels. You won't be able to eat just one.

1²/₃ cups confectioners' (powdered) sugar plus additional for dusting

½ cup plus 1 tablespoon all-purpose flour

½ cup almond flour or finely ground almonds

6 large egg whites

13 tablespoons unsalted butter, melted

1 tablespoon honey
Finely grated zest of 1 lemon

1 teaspoon freshly squeezed lemon juice

1. Grease a 12-cup muffin tin; set aside. In a bowl, combine the sugar, all-purpose flour, and almond flour. In the bowl of an electric mixer, whisk the egg whites until frothy. Slowly whisk in the sugar mixture. Whisk in the melted butter, the honey, lemon zest, and lemon juice.

2. Divide the batter among the muffin cups. Refrigerate for 1 hour.

3. Preheat oven to 375°F. Bake for 15 to 17 minutes or until dark golden around the edges and firm to the touch. Immediately remove the cakes from the muffin tin and transfer to a wire rack to cool. Dust cakes with additional confectioners' sugar just before serving.

makes 12 mini cakes

"The little cakes will suit you to a t!"— JAMIE

Elvis' Favorite Tea Sandwich

This peanut butter and banana sandwich is so sticky and satisfying, it's hard to imagine adding anything to it. But rumor has it Elvis used to tuck a few slices of crispy bacon under the bread—leave it to the King!

8   slices whole wheat bread
1   banana, peeled and cut into
      12 slices
½   cup peanut butter
1   tablespoon honey
1   tablespoon unsalted butter,
      melted

1. Using a 1¼-inch round cookie cutter, punch 3 circles out of each slice of bread. Spread 12 of the circles with 1 teaspoon peanut butter each. Place a banana slice on top of each peanut butter circle and mash slightly with a fork. Drizzle each banana slice with some honey. Top with the remaining 12 bread circles.

2. Preheat broiler. Transfer the sandwiches to a baking sheet. Brush the tops of the sandwiches with melted butter. Broil about 1 minute or until just golden.

makes 12 sandwiches to serve 4

"Here's snack time fit for a king." — BOBBY

LYNCHBURG CAKE & CANDY CO.
LYNCHBURG, TENNESSEE

About an hour from Nashville is a lovely little town called Lynchburg, population 361. As soon as we heard that a man there puts cake and whiskey together in one dessert, we decided it should be called Heaven. And we figured we should trot on over for a taste.

Billy Thomas, a retired Jack Daniel's distillery accountant and owner of Lynchburg Cake & Candy Co., breeds champion Tennessee walking horses when he's not pouring whiskey on cake. Mr. Thomas' 93-year-old mother, Bunt Thomas, taught him how to make her mother's traditional fruitcake. She claims the recipe is more than 135 years old. But it really came into its own when Billy got a hold of it. In true accountant fashion, Mr. Thomas precisely weighs all the ingredients for his batter on a kitchen scale before adding carefully premixed spices. The cakes bake up dense and spicy smelling. Then comes the magic: He pours Jack Daniel's right on top of every cake.

Once the loaves soak up their nice little drink, they're moist, spicy, and really pack a punch—you get the full force of the whiskey, but you can still taste every other ingredient. With all that booze, you can bet the cakes keep well, so they're perfect holiday gifts. Luckily Mr. Thomas bakes 36 cakes at a time in his home oven. We say, keep 'em coming!

Whiskey-Glazed Pork Loin

Visiting the home of Jack Daniel's taught us some very important lessons. Like: Everything tastes better with a little whiskey in it! You can test our theory with this flavorful roast.

1	2½-pound pork loin
	Salt and freshly ground
	black pepper
¼	cup pure maple syrup
2	tablespoons Tennessee whiskey
1	teaspoon dry mustard powder

1. Preheat oven to 400°F. Line a roasting pan with foil. Season the pork with salt and pepper; place in the prepared pan.

2. In a small bowl, whisk together the maple syrup, whiskey, and mustard powder. Brush the pork with half of the glaze. Roast about 1 hour and 15 minutes or until internal temperature of pork reaches 150°F, brushing with the remaining glaze after 45 minutes. Let the pork rest for 10 minutes before slicing.

makes 4 to 6 servings

Mint Juleps

If you say "whiskey" to a couple of Savannah boys like us, we think "mint julep." Here's our recipe for Derby day—and any other day you might find yourself thirsty for a cool, refreshing cocktail.

1	bunch fresh mint
4	teaspoons superfine sugar
4	teaspoons water
8	ounces (1 cup) Tennessee whiskey

1. Reserve four big sprigs of mint for garnish. Fill three ice cube trays with the remaining mint leaves (two leaves per compartment). Top leaves with water and freeze.

2. In each of four 10-ounce highball glasses, put 1 teaspoon sugar and 1 teaspoon water; stir until sugar is dissolved. Crush the mint ice by putting it inside a clean kitchen towel and pounding with a hammer. Divide the ice among the glasses. Pour 2 ounces of whiskey into each glass. Stir and serve garnished with the reserved mint sprigs.

makes 4 servings

Tennessee Whiskey Fruit and Nut Bars

We love to make bars because they come together faster than cookies, and you can pack even more good stuff into them. Here we add a generous dose of good ol' Tennessee whiskey.

BARS:

1½	cups all-purpose flour
¾	teaspoon baking powder
¼	teaspoon salt
⅔	cup butter, softened
¾	cup packed brown sugar
1½	teaspoons vanilla
2	large eggs
⅓	cup Tennessee whiskey
1	cup chopped pecans, toasted
½	cup golden raisins, candied ginger, dried cherries, or a combination
½	cup semisweet chocolate chips

FROSTING:

3½	cups confectioners' (powdered) sugar
6	tablespoons butter, softened
3	tablespoons Tennessee whiskey
1	teaspoon vanilla
24	pecan halves (optional)

1. Preheat oven to 350°F. Grease a 9×13-inch baking pan; set aside.

2. For the bars, in a bowl, combine flour, baking powder, and salt. With an electric mixer, cream together the ⅔ cup butter, the brown sugar, and 1½ teaspoons vanilla until fluffy. Beat in the eggs, one at a time. Alternately add the flour mixture and the ⅓ cup whiskey in three additions, mixing until fully combined after each addition. Fold in chopped nuts, the raisins, and chocolate chips. Spread the batter in the prepared pan. Bake for 20 to 25 minutes or until a toothpick inserted in the center comes out clean. Let bars cool in the pan on a wire rack.

3. For the frosting, in a large bowl, beat together the confectioners' sugar, the 6 tablespoons butter, 3 tablespoons whiskey, and 1 teaspoon vanilla until smooth. Add additional whiskey, if necessary, to make a frosting of spreadable consistency. Spread the frosting over the cooled bars. Cut into squares and, if desired, top each square with a pecan half.

makes 24 bars

"This high-proof cake is for grown-ups only." — BOBBY

NEELY'S
BAR-B-QUE
NASHVILLE, TENNESSEE

We weren't surprised to find Pat Neely in front of a big outdoor grill. It's his favorite spot, lucky for his customers. Pat went into the restaurant business with three brothers—Gaelin, Tony, and Mark—and his wife, Gina, in 1988. After building two successful restaurants in Memphis, they took on Nashville in 2001.

Pat says that with a family of five sons, his mama always had a big pot cooking in the kitchen. The boys learned to cook by standing around asking questions.

The Neely brothers use a dry rub and a barbecue sauce as the base of their popular barbecue. As for their secret? Well, Pat says pork is king in Tennessee, there are about 30 ingredients in the sauce, and no pit master

worth his salt would share his recipe!

Pat was happy to show us the innovations that help Neely's Bar-B-Que stand out in a town where barbecue is big. He makes a pasta dish by adding pulled pork to a large pot of simmering barbecue sauce, then tossing in spaghetti. The Neely brothers knew this dish was bound for glory, but at first they had a hard time convincing customers. "People were saying, 'Barbecued spaghetti? Those Neely boys have lost their minds!'"

Now each restaurant goes through about 80 gallons of barbecue spaghetti sauce a week. Unlike the pasta, the barbecue nachos were never a hard sell. Chips, pulled pork, barbecue sauce, cheese, and a sprinkling of Neely's dry rub—what's not to love?

The Deen Brothers' BBQ Chicken

Tennessee barbecue usually means pork: pork shoulder, ribs, or the whole hog. But where we come from, it means a great sauce, like this one, and good old chicken, the mainstay of our family business.

1   cup ketchup
1/4 cup packed dark brown sugar
2   tablespoons orange juice
1   teaspoon Worcestershire sauce
1   teaspoon liquid smoke
1/2 teaspoon dry mustard powder
1/4 teaspoon cayenne pepper
1   3½-pound chicken, cut
      into 8 pieces

1. Preheat oven to 375°F or prepare a grill (brush the grill grate lightly with oil).

2. In a large bowl, stir together all ingredients except the chicken. Reserve ⅓ cup of the barbecue sauce; set aside. Add the chicken to the remaining sauce in the bowl, turning to coat.

3. Arrange the coated chicken in a roasting pan or on the grill. Cook (covered, if grilling) for 40 to 45 minutes or until cooked through, basting with the reserved ⅓ cup sauce after 20 minutes.

makes 3 to 4 servings

"Grab the napkins, the bbq chicken's on the grill." — BOBBY

< Corn Bread Casserole with Pickled Jalapeños

We just love to put whole kernels in our corn bread. Here the sweet, golden little bites combine with piquant slices of jalapeño for a very exciting dish.

1	15½-ounce can whole kernel corn, drained
1	15-ounce can cream-style corn
1	8-ounce package corn muffin mix
1	cup sour cream
½	cup (1 stick) unsalted butter, melted
¼	cup sliced pickled jalapeños Pinch salt

1. Preheat oven to 350°F. Grease a 9-inch square baking pan;* set aside.

2. In a large bowl, stir together the whole corn, creamed corn, muffin mix, sour cream, butter, jalapeños, and salt. Pour batter into the prepared pan. Bake for 45 to 60 minutes or until a toothpick inserted in the center comes out clean.

*If desired, pour batter evenly into eight 6- to 8-ounce ramekins. Bake for 40 to 45 minutes.

makes 6 to 8 servings

Chipotle Collard Greens

When Tabasco started making chipotle hot pepper sauce, we started using it to spike up our regular recipe for collards. It's a match made in heaven.

2	large bunches collard greens (about 2 pounds), ribs removed
2	tablespoons unsalted butter
1	onion, halved and sliced
2	cloves garlic, chopped
2	cups water
1	to 2 teaspoons chipotle hot pepper sauce
½	teaspoon salt

1. Stack the collard greens and roll up the stack. Cut the roll into ½-inch-thick slices. Set aside.

2. In a medium pot, melt the butter over medium-high heat. Add the onion; saute about 5 minutes or until golden. Reduce heat to medium. Add the garlic; saute for 5 minutes more.

3. Add the water and collard greens to the pot; season with hot sauce and salt. Cook, uncovered, for 25 minutes, tossing the greens occasionally. Taste and adjust seasonings, if necessary.

makes 4 to 6 servings

BUTTERS BROWNIES
AUSTIN, TEXAS

With a name like Mary Louise Butters, it is no surprise that Mary Louise felt inspired to bake. Eventually. But first, in typical Austin style, she felt inspired to do everything from ballet to fiber arts. After living the life of a starving artist, Mary Louise headed into the kitchen and decided to "live life more sweetly" (her company motto) by opening Butters Brownies.

"Sweet" may not be the best word to describe her brownies, especially the rich, spicy ones she flavors with chipotle chiles, and the bags of dark, chewy brownie ends she calls "brownie butts" (with a vintage illustration of a lady's behind on the packaging). We were dying to taste her highly popular products, and she very sweetly showed us just how she makes them.

Mary Louise's basic brownies are loaded up with as much deep, dark, premium-quality chocolate as possible. The magic comes when Mary Louise marries the chocolate batter with another flavor. We juiced fresh ginger to make her zingy ginger brownies. We pureed chipotle chiles for the Aztec God brownies that Mary Louise claims capture the ancient combination of chocolate and chile. Then we tried the rose water brownies, which have a light, flowery scent. Sitting in Mary Louise's beautiful garden with a plate of her rose-flavored brownies was like heaven on earth. We believe she has found her true calling.

Brownie Cakes with Rose Whipped Cream

We add rose whipped cream to chewy-moist brownie baby cakes, which you can serve warm from the oven or after they've cooled down—if you can wait that long.

BROWNIES:

1	cup (2 sticks) plus 2 tablespoons unsalted butter
3	ounces chopped unsweetened chocolate
$\frac{1}{2}$	cup plus 1 tablespoon unsweetened cocoa powder
$2\frac{1}{2}$	cups granulated sugar
3	large eggs, at room temperature
1	tablespoon vanilla
$1\frac{1}{2}$	cups all-purpose flour
$\frac{1}{2}$	teaspoon salt

ROSE WHIPPED CREAM:

$1\frac{1}{2}$	cups heavy cream
1	tablespoon confectioners' (powdered) sugar
2	teaspoons rose water (or more to taste)

1. Preheat oven to 350°F. Spray 18 muffin cups with nonstick cooking spray; set aside.

2. In a double boiler or a microwave set on low power, melt the butter and chocolate, stirring frequently. Transfer chocolate mixture to a large bowl and let cool. Whisk in the cocoa until smooth. Whisk in the granulated sugar. Whisk in the eggs and vanilla. Fold in the flour and salt until just blended. (Do not overmix.)

3. Divide the batter evenly among the prepared muffin cups.* Bake about 12 minutes or until brownies are slightly underdone (they should be gooey inside). Let cool in pan on a wire rack for 5 minutes.

4. While the brownies bake, whip the cream and confectioners' sugar together until soft peaks form (tips curl). Stir in the rose water. Serve the brownie cakes warm with a dollop of whipped cream.

*If you have to use part of a 12-cup muffin pan to make up the 18 cups needed, spoon a little water into the empty cups to allow the heat to distribute evenly across the pan.

makes 18 brownies

Espresso Brownies

We came up with these brownies spiked with espresso especially for grown-ups. They sure do make a person feel greedy.

ESPRESSO BROWNIES:

12	ounces semisweet chocolate chips
2	ounces bittersweet chocolate, chopped
¼	cup (½ stick) unsalted butter
1½	cups all-purpose flour
3	tablespoons unsweetened cocoa powder
1	teaspoon baking powder
¼	teaspoon salt
2	tablespoons instant espresso powder
1¼	cups granulated sugar
3	eggs
2	teaspoons vanilla

FROSTING:

6	tablespoons unsalted butter
1	pound sifted confectioners' (powdered) sugar
3	tablespoons unsweetened cocoa powder
3	tablespoons coffee-flavored liqueur
1	teaspoon instant espresso powder dissolved in 1 tablespoon boiling water
2	teaspoons milk

1. Preheat oven to 350°F. Grease a 9-inch square baking pan; set aside.

2. In a double boiler or a microwave set on low power, melt the chocolates and ¼ cup butter, stirring frequently; set aside. In a large bowl, sift together the flour, 3 tablespoons cocoa, the baking powder, salt, and 2 tablespoons espresso powder. In the bowl of an electric mixer, beat granulated sugar, eggs, and vanilla on medium-high speed for 2 to 3 minutes or until light colored. Add the melted chocolate mixture; beat until combined. Gradually add the flour mixture; mix until blended.

3. Pour the batter into the prepared pan. Bake for 35 to 40 minutes or until a toothpick inserted in the center comes out mostly clean (these brownies should be fudgy in the center). Cool completely in pan on a wire rack.

4. For the frosting, in the bowl of an electric mixer, cream together the 6 tablespoons butter and the confectioners' sugar. Add the 3 tablespoons cocoa, the liqueur, espresso, and milk; beat until smooth. Use a spatula to spread the frosting over the brownies. Cut the brownies into squares.

makes 16 squares

~~Royers Round Top Café~~

Website: www.royersroundtopcafe.com e-mail: pieman@royersroundtopcafe.com
1-877-866-pies (7437) * 979-249-3611 * On The Square * Round Top, Texas
Hours: Thursday 11-9 * Friday and Saturday 11-9:30 & Sunday 11-3
(Open 'til 7 on Sunday from March 19 to August 15)

All of our entrees, EXCEPT pastas, come with a choice of two veggies: black-eyed peas with tomatoes, mashed potato casserole, creamed-corn, or cold broccoli salad. For $1.50 you can order a dinner salad as one of your veggies. Feel free to order an extra vegetable for an extra $1.50. Or you can substitute the veggies for Pasta & stir-fry veggies for $3.50, Micah's Pasta for $6.95, or another pasta of your choice (prices will vary). OMG—"Oh My God!" is our classification of certain menu items. It is what your taste buds say when you take a bite into one of these dishes.

<u>NOTE FOR VEGETARIANS</u>—We can prepare any of our pastas without the meat and we can fix wonderful salads with field green lettuces. Please let us know if you have any special dietary needs before you place your order. We'll do our best to accommodate your needs.

~~OH HOW 'BOUT SOME APPETIZERS?~~

CAFÉ'S JALAPENO-SOURDOUGH BREAD GRILLED SHRIMP BLT OMG!
Defines a sandwich! A ¼ pound of shrimp, BLT with our smokin' mesquite mustard $11.95

CHICKEN CORN CHOWDER WITH CILANTRO
The flavor is out of this world! Served with jalapeno sourdough bread.
Mug $3.50   Bowl $4.50

JALAPENO CHEESE SOUP
wow...won't blow you away but has a kick to it! Served with jalapeno sourdough bread.
Mug $3.50   Bowl $4.50

REALLY BIG STUFFED JALAPENOS OMG X2
stuffed with Swiss, cheddar & cream cheese with crabmeat & shrimp stuffing. Served with our cilantro-ranch dressing
2--$6.95 or 4--$11.95

GRILLED QUAIL (whole bird)
Our *succulent and tender* quail; cut in half, serves two. $4.95

SHRIMP STUFFED GRILLED QUAIL
Our boneless quail, stuffed with shrimp & cilantro, wrapped around bacon then grilled.
$9.95

SOME STUFF THAT MOO

THE GREAT STEAK OMG x 4
Our customers say, "It is the best steak they have ever eaten!" A 10oz center-cut filet, that can be cut with your fork & definitely shouldn't be cooked beyond medium. $31.95 (worth every penny).

BEEF TENDERLOIN PLATE
Sliced beef grilled & topped with grilled onions & melted swiss with a side of horseradish dressing. $15.95

SOME STUFF THAT SWIM

MICAH'S SNAPPER OMG X 3
A WOW DISH!! Grilled gulf red snapper topped with shrimp sautéed in white wine, olive oil, basil, garlic & tomatoes. $22.95

TARA's GRILLED GULF RED SNAPPER OMG
Simply, this is our finest fish! $17.95

"A MEAL TO REMEMBER" OMG x 2
Grilled gulf red snapper with a side of Micah's pasta. *A GREAT MEAL!* $21.95

FRESH GRILLED SALMON
The Gurry's Special A grilled fresh filet. Simple and flavorful! $16.95

MICAH'S SALMON OMG X 2
A WOW DISH!!! Grilled salmon topped with shrimp sautéed in white wine, olive oil, basil, garlic & tomatoes. $20.95

JUST FOR KIDS!!
FOR KIDS 10 & UNDER...PLEASE DO NOT EVEN ASK! We'll ask to see your driver's license with and show off your great photo off to the dining room!

CHICKEN FINGERS
3 fingers, 2 veggies & a soda

SOME STUFF THAT OINK & CHIRP

TODD'S PORK TENDERLOIN OMG x 3
Truly an awesome pork dish! A 10 oz. grilled pork tenderloin, topped with our peach & pepper glaze! OH SO GOOD! $17.95

GRILLED PORK CHOP
A 14oz. center cut pork chop topped with grilled onions and served with roasted raspberry chipolte sauce $15.95

GRILLED QUAIL (WHOLE BIRD) OMG!
Succulent & tender! No Buckshot!
2- 15.95 or 3- 20.95 each additional 4.95

SHRIMP STUFFED GRILLED QUAIL OMG x2
An unbelievable combination of flavors! A whole boneless quail stuffed with grilled shrimp & cilantro, wrapped in bacon & grilled.
1 - $14.95 or 2- $23.95 each additional $8.95

QUAIL COMBO
Can't decide on what quail to get? Try 1 of each. $19.95

"L.I.T.S."-Life Is Too Short Special OMG x 3
For those who cannot decide. A side of angus pasta, a portion of the grilled pork tenderloin served with the peach and pepper glaze & a grilled quail $18.95 or with a stuffed quail $23.95

KAREN'S LEMON CHEST (OMG x -3).
A chest of chicken dipped in fresh lemon juice & battered in Parmesan cheese & then fried $10.95

FUNKY CHICKEN
A grilled chicken breast topped with grilled onions and bleu cheese dressing $10.95

SOME STUFF IN A BOWL—

MICAH'S PASTA—OMG!
Our first "light" dish! Shrimp sautéed in olive oil, white wine,

ROYERS ROUND TOP CAFE
ROUND TOP, TEXAS

Halfway between Austin and Houston in Round Top, Texas (population 73), we met up with Bud Royer, "the pie man," to talk pie. We had heard that folks regularly drive from Austin, Houston, and even San Antonio to eat at the Royer family's roadside cafe.

Bud started serving his chocolate chip pie in a handmade crust when he and his wife bought the cafe in 1987, and it was so popular in the first year that he hired another employee just to make pie. Almost overnight his chocolate chip pie became 10 times as popular. The woman Bud hired had made a mistake and doubled about half of the ingredients, magically taking Bud's pie from good to out-of-this-world great, like the world's best chewy chocolate chip cookie in pie form.

You can order the pie warm with a scoop of vanilla ice cream, or you can have it plain, but that costs 50 cents extra because Bud believes ice cream on pie makes a good thing better. He sure made a good thing better when he took over the cafe and then when he changed the recipe for his chocolate chip pie. Of course, once you have found that magic formula, the trick is to keep it up. Lucky for Texas, Royers Round Top Cafe, now run by Bud's daughter, Tara, is sticking to its great food and unforgettable pie. The rest of us can order his pies—or get into our kitchens and work our own magic.

< Shrimp Salad Sandwiches

Royers Round Top Cafe serves some pretty gourmet food, like shrimp BLTs on jalapeño sourdough. Just as intriguing is our sandwich, where flavorful fresh shrimp get spruced up with bacon, jalapeños, and a lemony mayo dressing.

½ cup mayonnaise
1 tablespoon freshly squeezed
   lemon juice
1 to 2 pickled jalapeños, seeded and
   finely chopped
1 pound cooked and peeled shrimp,
   coarsely chopped
8 slices bacon, cooked and crumbled
   Salt and freshly ground
   black pepper
8 slices challah bread, toasted
4 leaves red leaf lettuce
4 slices tomato (8 slices if tomatoes
   are small)

1. In a medium bowl, stir together the mayonnaise, lemon juice, and jalapeño. Add the shrimp and bacon; toss to combine. Season to taste with salt and pepper.

2. Spread the shrimp salad evenly on 4 slices of bread. Top with lettuce, tomato, and the remaining slices of bread.

makes 4 servings

Creamed Corn and Fried Onion Casserole

This is the kind of down-home casserole that makes everyone at a potluck come running, begging for the recipe. Here it is, and it couldn't be simpler.

1 8-ounce package cream cheese
1 10-ounce package frozen corn,
   thawed
   Salt and freshly ground
   black pepper
1 cup canned french-fried onions

1. Preheat oven to 350°F. Grease a 7-inch square baking pan or casserole dish. Spread the cream cheese evenly on the bottom of the pan. Top with corn, pressing the corn into the cheese. Season to taste with salt and pepper. Spread the onions evenly over the top. Bake for 30 minutes.

makes 4 to 6 servings

Chocolate Chip Pie

Here's our slightly simpler version of Bud's fantastic pie (which you should mail-order if you love gooey chocolate chip cookies). Chocolate chip whipped cream is a pretty good substitute for the ice cream Bud insists you eat with it.

PIE:

2³⁄₄	cups all-purpose flour
1¹⁄₂	teaspoons salt
1¹⁄₄	teaspoons baking soda
1	teaspoon baking powder
1	cup (2 sticks) unsalted butter, softened
1¹⁄₂	cups packed light brown sugar
¹⁄₂	cup granulated sugar
3	large eggs
1	tablespoon vanilla
3	cups semisweet chocolate chips
2	cups chopped walnuts (optional)

WHIPPED CREAM:

2	pints (4 cups) heavy cream
¹⁄₄	cup confectioners' (powdered) sugar
¹⁄₂	cup miniature semisweet chocolate chips

1. Preheat oven to 350°F. Grease two 9-inch pie plates; set aside.

2. In a large bowl, sift together the flour, salt, baking soda, and baking powder. In the bowl of an electric mixer, cream together butter, brown sugar, and granulated sugar. Add the eggs, one at a time, beating until incorporated. Beat in the vanilla. Add flour mixture, a little at a time, and mix until fully combined. Fold in the 3 cups chocolate chips and, if desired, the walnuts. Divide the dough between the prepared pie plates and smooth the tops with a spatula.

3. Bake about 30 minutes or until pies are golden and slightly firm to the touch but still soft. If the pies begin to darken too much before they are baked through, cover with foil and continue baking. Let pies cool completely on a wire rack.

4. While the pies cool, whip the cream until soft peaks form (tips curl). Add the confectioners' sugar and whip until just combined. Fold in the chocolate chips. Refrigerate whipped cream until ready to use. Spread the whipped cream over the pies and serve.

makes 12 to 16 servings

LIVE MUSIC ★ AND ★ LEGENDARY BAR-B-Q

THE COUNTY LINE
AUSTIN, TEXAS

Skeeter Miller and his buddies went into the barbecue business 30 years ago, and as Skeeter puts it, the keys to great 'cue are the best meat and 18 to 20 hours in the smoker—a long time to wait for dinner. Luckily we didn't have to wait quite so long. In fact The County Line can smoke 3,500 pounds of meat in each of its three steel smoker pits, so you can always find some tender Angus beef ribs and tangy, citrus-glazed baby back pork ready to eat.

We helped Skeeter make up a batch of basic barbecue sauce from the usual suspects: onion, molasses, ketchup, vinegar, mustard, Worcestershire, and lime juice. For the pork glaze, we took that sauce and added brown sugar and orange juice, then brushed it on the meat right before it was done, just in time to caramelize and flavor the pork.

We passed the margarita machine on the way into the dining room, which prompted Skeeter to tell us the history of the place. It was a speakeasy in the 1920s, full of liquor, women, and politicians breaking their own laws. Nowadays the liquor is legal, but there ought to be a law against barbecue this good. They have an all-you-can-eat menu and another called all-you-can-stand. We tried the homemade bread, coleslaw, beans, and potato salad and polished off as much of that rich, tasty beef and smoky glazed pork as possible. That was a meal worth waiting for.

Dry-Rub Baby Back Ribs

We love ribs so much we had to come up with a recipe that was easy enough—and delicious enough—to make every time we have a craving, and this one fits the bill.

1	tablespoon paprika
1½	teaspoons packed dark brown sugar
1½	teaspoons finely grated orange zest
1½	teaspoons salt
¾	teaspoon ground cumin
½	teaspoon ground black pepper
¼	teaspoon cayenne pepper (or to taste)
4	pounds baby back ribs, cut into 2-rib portions

1. In a small bowl, stir together all ingredients except the ribs. Rub spice mixture all over the ribs. Cover and refrigerate ribs for at least 2 hours or up to 24 hours.

2. Preheat oven to 400°F. Place the ribs in a roasting pan. Bake for 1 hour.

makes 6 servings

Texas Margaritas >

Tequila and beer make these slushy, orange- and lime-flavored drinks pack a Texas-size punch. They're just the thing on a blazing-hot summer night.

6 ounces (¾ cup) frozen limeade concentrate
6 ounces (¾ cup) tequila
4 ounces (½ cup) beer
2 ounces (¼ cup) orange juice
2 cups ice cubes
Coarse salt (optional)

1. In a blender, combine all ingredients except salt. Blend on high until smooth and slushy. Serve in salt-rimmed glasses, if desired.

makes 4 (8-ounce) drinks

Bacon-Wrapped Corn on the Cob

We have found that bacon gives the corn a nice smoky flavor, but it doesn't get brown and crispy. You can either eat it with the corn or peel it off.

4 ears corn, unhusked
4 slices bacon
Freshly ground black pepper

1. Prepare a grill for low direct heat.

2. Peel back the cornhusks but do not remove them. Pull out and discard all the silk. Working from top to bottom, wrap a strip of bacon in a spiral around each ear of corn. Season with pepper. Pull the husk back over the corn. Wrap a piece of foil tightly around the top 1½ inches of the ear of corn. (Or use a piece of kitchen twine soaked in water to tie the tops of the cornhusks closed.)

3. Grill the corn about 10 minutes or until the husks are brown all over, turning occasionally. Let corn cool for 5 minutes before serving.

makes 4 servings

The West

COLORADO

The Rocky Mountains meet the Great Plains in Boulder, Colorado. With its fantastic views and fresh air, Boulder is consistently voted among the most livable cities in the country. The surrounding 30,000 acres of natural beauty are heaven for hikers, bikers, skiers, and rock climbers, but foodies shouldn't overlook Boulder either. We hiked up a mountain (well, our car did!) to get to a restaurant where we could enjoy Colorado lamb three different ways on one plate. Then we checked out the incredible chocolates and baked goods this creative city has to offer.

CALIFORNIA

California means beautiful sun-bathed beaches, rolling hills of vineyards, and fit people—everywhere we looked, someone was surfing or biking. Even the dogs go jogging there. Alongside those great beaches and wineries are some wonderful restaurants and markets. And while you might think of California as one big salad bowl since everyone looks so healthy and most of the country's produce is grown here, we found all kinds of unforgettable food up and down the West Coast, from seafood stew to saltwater taffy to the country's only wine grape pie.

WASHINGTON

They call Seattle the Emerald City, and when we got there we knew we weren't in Kansas (or Savannah) anymore. Things looked, felt, sounded, and smelled different. You could smell coffee roasting everywhere, you could hear folks making all kinds of music indoors and out, and you could plug in a laptop computer just about anywhere—even in the park! This quirky, hip, charming, and surprising city is home to an enormous sculpture of a troll, the very first Starbucks (open since 1971), and Pike Place, the country's oldest continuously operating farmer's market. Full of young energy, innovative spirit, and strong coffee, Seattle is a happening place.

FLAGSTAFF HOUSE RESTAURANT
BOULDER, COLORADO

The cooking at the historic Flagstaff House has to be good—it competes with the spectacular views from the dining room. Five minutes out of Boulder, overlooking the city and the Rockies, Flagstaff House has been in the Monette family since 1971, and the restaurant just keeps getting better.

While chef Mark Monette dishes up fine favorites like his amazing local Colorado lamb made three ways, his brother Scott manages the restaurant. Their story was familiar to us, but the food at Flagstaff is a far cry from our down-home fried chicken specialties.

Mark said that 80 percent of the lamb purchased in America is Colorado lamb—it is bigger and fresher than New Zealand lamb, with great flavor. Mark selects the three best cuts of grass-fed Colorado lamb—the shank, rack, and loin—and treats each one differently, marinating the shank, then braising it until it is fall-apart tender, roasting the lamb rack with a mustard and rosemary crust, and flavoring the tender lamb loin with olive oil, rosemary, and garlic.

Mark arranges the plate so beautifully, placing the lamb alongside truffled polenta and ratatouille, that it doesn't matter if the sun is setting on the mountains outside the windows. We sat down with a wine from Flagstaff's awardwinning cellar and a plate of Mark's tender, juicy lamb, and we hardly looked up. That was definitely the best dinner we've ever had away from Mama's table—even if you don't count the view.

Grilled Rosemary Lamb Chops >

We learned a lot about lamb in Colorado—the biggest lesson being just how delicious lamb could be! We created these marinated chops and have been grilling them ever since we got back.

2	pounds lamb rib chops
	Salt and freshly ground black pepper
2	tablespoons olive oil
1	tablespoon chopped fresh rosemary
2	teaspoons chopped garlic

1. Season the lamb chops with salt and pepper. In a large bowl, stir together the oil, rosemary, and garlic. Add lamb chops, turning to coat. Cover and refrigerate for at least 2 hours or up to 24 hours.

2. Prepare a grill or preheat the broiler. Grill or broil chops to desired doneness (about 6 minutes for rare, 7 minutes for medium rare), turning chops so they brown well on all sides.

makes 4 servings

Goat Cheese Grits >

We love gourmet and imported foods, but most nights, we would just as soon tuck into a big bowl of cheese grits. So we dressed these grits up with goat cheese to make them a great match with grilled lamb.

2	cups milk
2	cups water
2	tablespoons unsalted butter
1¼	teaspoons salt
1	cup yellow or white grits (not instant)
2	ounces soft goat cheese (about ½ cup)

1. In a saucepan, combine milk, water, butter, and salt; bring to a boil. Stir in the grits. Reduce heat to low; cook about 15 minutes or until thickened, stirring often. Stir in the goat cheese. Serve immediately.

makes 4 servings

Ratatouille Supreme with Pepper Jack

This is ratatouille made casserole-style, with a healthy topping of peppery cheese. We think it's a great improvement on the original, if we do say so ourselves.

1	small baguette, cut into ¼-inch-thick slices
6	tablespoons olive oil
3	large onions, sliced
6	cloves garlic (5 chopped, 1 whole)
2	pounds eggplant, trimmed and cubed
1	pound zucchini or yellow squash, trimmed and cubed
1	pound cherry tomatoes, halved
1	large sprig fresh rosemary
1¼	teaspoons salt
½	teaspoon freshly ground black pepper
½	cup fresh basil leaves, chopped
2	teaspoons freshly squeezed lemon juice
1	teaspoon chopped fresh rosemary leaves
	Olive oil for brushing
2	cups shredded pepper Jack cheese

1. Preheat oven to 400°F. Arrange the baguette slices in a single layer on a baking sheet. Toast in oven for 3 to 5 minutes or until pale golden. Set aside.

2. In a large skillet, heat 3 tablespoons of the oil over medium heat. Add the onions; cook for 15 to 20 minutes or until golden, stirring occasionally. Add the chopped garlic; cook for 30 seconds. Stir in the remaining 3 tablespoons oil, the eggplant, zucchini, tomatoes, rosemary sprig, salt, and pepper. Cook and stir for 5 minutes. Cover and reduce heat to low. Cook about 25 minutes more or until vegetables are fork-tender.

3. While the mixture cooks, chop the remaining garlic clove; set aside. Uncover the pan and increase heat to medium-high. Cook about 10 minutes or until the mixture thickens. Remove the rosemary sprig. Stir in the remaining garlic, the basil, lemon juice, and chopped rosemary.

4. Preheat the broiler. Transfer the vegetable mixture to a 2- to 3-quart casserole dish. Arrange the toasted baguette slices over top. Brush the bread with additional olive oil. Top evenly with pepper Jack cheese. Broil 4 to 5 inches from heat for 1 to 2 minutes or until the bread is golden and the cheese has melted.

makes 6 servings

WEN CHOCOLATES
WHEAT RIDGE, COLORADO

William Poole crafts fine chocolate truffles in a huge variety of innovative flavors, but he knew we would want to reach right for what he calls the Savannah truffle. We were curious about whether a guy in Colorado could turn our town into a truffle, so he showed us how he did it.

In addition to really good chocolate and fresh cream, Wen chocolates get a boost of flavor from fresh, exotic spices. We went with William to pick out a quartet of warm, savory ground peppers: white pepper, cayenne pepper, Aleppo pepper from Syria, and spicy Hungarian paprika. William simmered these in a pot of cream until the flavor was strong enough, then strained the heated cream onto his chocolate to melt it, stirred in some honey vodka to complement the spiciness, and poured the flavored mixture (which is called ganache) into little chocolate-lined molds. They are refrigerated until they set.

To finish the truffles, William sprinkled each little truffle with a tiny shower of paprika, then capped it with two very thin slices of chile mango (mango slices dipped in chili powder). Those truffles were so pretty, but that didn't stop us from digging in. And we were amazed: The truffles tasted spicy and lively at first, but then smooth and lingering—just like Savannah! You just never know where you will find a taste of home.

The William Truffles

After meeting William at his chocolate shop, we invented a white chocolate and pecan truffle in his honor that is crusty on the outside but soft on the inside. This one's for you, William!

WHITE CHOCOLATE–PECAN FILLING:

½	cup heavy cream
12	ounces white chocolate
2	teaspoons vanilla
1½	cups finely chopped toasted pecans

CHOCOLATE COATING:

12	ounces bittersweet chocolate, chopped
1	tablespoon unsalted butter
4½	cups crisp rice cereal

1. In a saucepan, bring cream to a boil. Place the white chocolate in a large bowl and pour hot cream over the chocolate. Let stand for 1 minute, then gently whisk until smooth. Add vanilla and mix just until combined. Fold in chopped pecans. Refrigerate until cool and firm.

2. Remove the white chocolate mixture from the refrigerator. Using a teaspoon measure or melon baller, form mixture into ball-shape truffles. Place truffles on a baking sheet. Refrigerate about 30 minutes or until firm.

3. Remove the truffles from the refrigerator. In a double boiler or a microwave set on low power, melt the bittersweet chocolate and butter, stirring frequently. Let chocolate cool at room temperature for 2 minutes.

4. Place cereal in a shallow dish. Dip the truffles, one at a time, in the chocolate coating until completely covered, then roll the truffles in cereal. Let set at room temperature for at least 2 hours or chill for 15 minutes before serving.

makes about 20 truffles

Truffle Pie

The layers of chocolate in this pie are mind-boggling. We make it for dessert whenever we have chocoholics over. Remember to start making this the day before so the pie can firm up in the fridge.

TRUFFLE FILLING:

²⁄₃   cup heavy cream
6   ounces bittersweet
     chocolate chips

1   9-inch prepared graham
     cracker crust

WHIPPED CHOCOLATE FILLING:

6   ounces bittersweet
     chocolate chips
1½   cups heavy cream
½   teaspoon vanilla

WHIPPED CREAM TOPPING:

1   cup heavy cream
¼   cup confectioners'
     (powdered) sugar

GARNISH:

1½   ounces milk chocolate
1½   ounces white chocolate
1½   ounces semisweet or
     dark chocolate

1. For the truffle filling, in a saucepan, bring ²⁄₃ cup cream to a simmer. Place the 6 ounces chocolate chips in a bowl and pour the hot cream over the chocolate. Let stand for 1 minute, then gently whisk until smooth. Spread truffle filling over the bottom of the prepared piecrust. Freeze for 20 minutes.

2. Meanwhile, for the whipped chocolate filling, in a double boiler or a microwave set on low power, heat the 6 ounces chocolate chips with ½ cup of the cream until the chocolate is just melted, stirring often. Let cool to room temperature. In a chilled bowl, beat the remaining 1 cup cream until thick. Add the chocolate mixture and the vanilla and beat until soft peaks form (tips curl). Spread the whipped chocolate mixture over the truffle filling in the crust. Refrigerate overnight.

3. Just before serving, for the topping, beat 1 cup cream on medium speed of an electric mixer until it begins to thicken. Add confectioners' sugar and whip until stiff peaks form (tips stand straight). Spread the whipped cream over the top of the pie. Using a grater or vegetable peeler, make pieces or shavings of milk chocolate, white chocolate, and semisweet or dark chocolate. Garnish pie with chocolate pieces. Serve immediately.

makes 8 servings

THE BOULDER DUSHANBE TEAHOUSE
BOULDER, COLORADO

We came to Boulder hoping for good food, and we ended up learning about Persian architecture too! When we got to The Boulder Dushanbe Teahouse to try its famous gingerbread, we found an ornate, intricately decorated teahouse waiting for us.

Lenny Martinelli, who runs the restaurant, explained that in 1987 the mayor of the capital of Tajikistan, Dushanbe, sent Boulder a teahouse to develop sister-city ties. This incredible structure, the handiwork of 40 artisans, arrived from the former USSR in 200 wooden crates. Once the building was finally put together, it became Boulder's most exotic and most beautiful structure. Currently the city of Boulder is reciprocating with a cybercafe in Dushanbe.

Amid the gorgeous, handpainted tiles there is a lot of serious tea to try, an international menu of great cooking, and a little cake called Tangerine Tea Gingerbread that outsells everything else. What makes this cake special? Tea, of course! Lenny brews an extra-dark cup of the house tangerine tea and adds it to a standard gingerbread recipe. Then he serves the cake with orange-caramel sauce and a five-spice whipped cream.

When we sat down to try this famous cake, Lenny poured the tea, filling our cups only halfway because in Tajikistan that means the host would like his guest to stay for more. Once we tasted that spicy, gingery cake with its mysterious taste of tea, we were in no hurry to leave.

Fish Fajitas

The Boulder Dushanbe Teahouse has one of the most eclectic menus we've ever seen, with items from Tabrizi Kooftah Balls (meatballs with dried fruit and nuts) to tasty fish tacos. Here is our version, made into fajitas.

1½	pounds mahi mahi or other firm-fleshed white fish fillets, skin removed
	Salt and freshly ground black pepper
1	tablespoon olive oil
8	8-inch flour tortillas
1	cup fresh salsa
1	avocado, peeled, pitted, and sliced
1	lime, cut into 8 wedges

1. Cut the fish into strips and season with salt and pepper. In a medium skillet, heat the oil over medium-high heat. Add fish; cook for 4 to 5 minutes or until cooked through, stirring frequently.

2. Heat a separate skillet (do not use nonstick) over medium-high heat. Warm the tortillas, one at a time, in the skillet. Line a plate or a wide, shallow bowl with a clean kitchen towel. Immediately transfer the hot tortillas to the plate, folding the edges of the towel over tortillas to keep them warm.

3. To assemble, divide the fish among tortillas and top with salsa and avocado slices. Squeeze lime juice over the avocado and roll up the tortillas.

makes 4 servings

< Hummus with Pita and Vegetables

If you've never made your own hummus, you're in for a treat. The blender does all the work, and the results are creamy and delicious. This is a favorite snack of ours.

2	15½-ounce cans chickpeas, drained (reserve ⅓ cup liquid)
⅓	cup olive oil
3	tablespoons freshly squeezed lemon juice
1	teaspoon tahini
½	teaspoon salt
1	clove garlic
	Freshly ground black pepper
	Pinch ground cumin
	Pita chips
	Raw veggies (carrots, celery, cucumber, bell pepper)

1. In a food processor, combine the chickpeas, oil, lemon juice, tahini, salt, garlic, and pepper to taste. Process until smooth, adding the reserved chickpea liquid as needed to reach desired consistency for dip.

2. Spread the hummus on a large plate. Sprinkle with cumin. Serve with pita chips and raw veggies for dipping.

makes 2 cups hummus

Upside-Down Pear Gingerbread

This is our quick fruit-filled twist on The Boulder Dushanbe Teahouse's excellent gingerbread. Sometimes we add a dollop of whipped cream.

1	tablespoon unsalted butter, softened
1	tablespoon packed dark brown sugar
1	15-ounce can pear halves, drained and sliced lengthwise
1	14½-ounce box gingerbread mix

1. Preheat oven to 350°F. Spread butter over the bottom and sides of an 8-inch square pan. Sprinkle brown sugar over bottom of pan. Lay the pear slices in one layer over the brown sugar.

2. Prepare the gingerbread mix according to package directions. Pour batter into the prepared pan. Bake for 35 to 40 minutes or until a toothpick inserted in the center comes out clean.

3. Cool in pan on a wire rack for 5 minutes. Run a sharp knife along the sides of the pan. Place a serving plate, upside down, over the top of the pan and invert the cake onto the plate.

makes 6 to 9 servings

SWEETIE PIES
NAPA, CALIFORNIA

Toni Chiapetta's Sweetie Pies bakery is as sweet as its name, with cases full of amazing pies, cakes, tarts, and cookies. Toni makes beautiful tarts piled high with gorgeous fruit, layer cakes loaded with creamy, buttery icing (just our style), and a pie that would even rival Mama's.

During the one-month grape harvest in the fall, Toni makes a Cabernet pie, and we were there at just the right time to give it a try. Toni took us to a vineyard to pick the fruit ourselves, where we learned that an experienced guy can pick a ton of grapes in a day. We needed only a few pounds for the pie, but it was clear we weren't up to speed! Back in the shop, Toni brought out her golden brown, all-butter piecrust, baked and ready to be filled with grapes, sugar, and some orange juice. That pie came together so fast, it made sense of the saying "easy as pie." The grapes cooked up into a delicious jamlike filling, and like many of our favorite recipes, the simplicity of this pie lets the ingredients shine. Back home, we used table grapes in some great recipes inspired by our visit to Sweetie Pies.

Grape, Blue Cheese, and Walnut Bites >

We love to serve these nibbles with a drink before dinner. The juicy grapes, salty cheese, and crunchy walnuts are an addictive combination.

30	walnut halves, toasted
¼	cup blue cheese
15	seedless red or green grapes, halved

1. Arrange the walnut halves on a platter, flat sides up. Spread a heaping ¼ teaspoon blue cheese on each walnut half. Top the cheese with a grape half.

makes 30 pieces

Two-Grape Custard Pie

Our pie is creamy from the custard and sweet and juicy from the grapes. It works well with only one kind of grape too.

CRUST:

1	cup all-purpose flour
½	teaspoon salt
⅓	cup cold unsalted butter or shortening (or a combination), cut into cubes
2	to 3 tablespoons cold water

FILLING:

1	cup seedless red grapes
1	cup seedless green grapes
2	tablespoons unsalted butter, melted
½	cup sugar
¼	cup all-purpose flour
¼	teaspoon salt
1	cup heavy cream
3	eggs
3	tablespoons brandy
1	teaspoon vanilla

1. For crust, combine 1 cup flour and ½ teaspoon salt. Cut in ⅓ cup butter until mixture forms large crumbs. Sprinkle in water, 1 tablespoon at a time, tossing gently with fork until dough comes together. Form dough into a disk, wrap in plastic, and refrigerate for 1 hour or up to 2 days.

2. Preheat oven to 375°F. For filling, toss grapes with 2 tablespoons butter; transfer to rimmed baking pan and set aside. On a floured surface, roll dough to an 11-inch circle. Transfer to a 9-inch pie plate; flute edges. Line crust with foil; fill with pie weights. Place the grapes and crust in the oven. After 20 minutes, remove the grapes. Remove foil and weights from crust; continue to bake crust for 5 to 10 minutes or until pale golden. Reduce oven temperature to 350°F.

3. Combine sugar, ¼ cup flour, and ¼ teaspoon salt. Whisk in cream and eggs until smooth. Stir in roasted grapes, brandy, and vanilla. Pour filling into hot crust. Bake for 25 to 30 minutes or until puffed and golden. Let pie cool at least 15 minutes before serving.

makes 8 servings

Roasted Lemon Chicken with Red Grapes

A good roast yard bird is so simple and delicious, you could make it for dinner every night. Sometimes we like to mix things up a bit, so we added lemon and grapes for a bright, tangy flavor in this recipe.

4   to 5 pounds chicken drumsticks
       and thighs (bone-in)
1   clove garlic, halved
4   tablespoons unsalted butter, melted
2   teaspoons finely grated lemon zest
2   tablespoons freshly squeezed
       lemon juice
     Salt and freshly ground
       black pepper
2   pounds seedless red grapes
1   teaspoon sugar

1. Preheat oven to 425°F. Rinse chicken and pat dry with paper towels. Rub the chicken pieces all over with the cut sides of the garlic clove. Place chicken in a large bowl.

2. In a small bowl, whisk together 2 tablespoons of the melted butter, the lemon zest, and lemon juice; season generously with salt and pepper. Pour the butter mixture over the chicken pieces and toss to coat.

3. In a separate bowl, toss together the grapes, the remaining 2 tablespoons melted butter, and the sugar. Season the grapes with salt and pepper. Arrange the grapes in the bottom of a 9×13-inch baking pan.

4. Place the chicken on top of the grapes. Roast, without turning, for 40 to 45 minutes or until chicken is cooked through and the juices run clear when chicken is pricked with a fork.

makes 4 to 6 servings

"Red grapes add juicy sweetness to this dinnertime favorite. My boys did good!" — PAULA

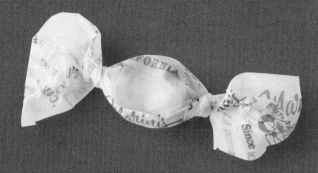

MARINI'S CANDIES
SANTA CRUZ, CALIFORNIA

To find Marini's Candies in Santa Cruz, just look for the Ferris wheel. As soon as we hit that beachside amusement park, we felt like boys gone wild! Joe Marini is the fourth generation in his family's business, which began in 1915 with Victor Marini's popcorn stand. The shop is right on the boardwalk (one of the last remaining on the West Coast) and is a veritable candy land complete with simmering copper kettles turning out classic sweets such as saltwater taffy, candy apples, caramel corn, buttery peanut brittle, and irresistible fudge.

In the front window, an antique machine pulls big, thick ropes of taffy, either plain white or pastel colored depending on the flavor. We were mesmerized, watching the sticky candy turn light and airy, get fed into the wrapping machine in a long strand, and finally come out the other end in neatly wrapped little bites. The taffy is still made from Victor's recipe, and the wrapping machine dates back to 1920. Joe explained that they could use a faster machine, but it wouldn't be as fun to watch!

We especially loved the cherry-, molasses-, and peanut butter-flavored taffy. The shop makes great hand-dipped chocolates too, and its turtles are just about as nice as the ones we get in Georgia. All those sticky treats left us in the mood for some good Southern divinity.

Brown Sugar Divinity

Brown sugar is our twist on good, old-fashioned Southern divinity. This is one of those recipes that we make when we're craving a taste of home sweet home—and it makes a great gift too.

1	cup packed light brown sugar
1	cup granulated sugar
⅔	cup water
⅓	cup light corn syrup
⅛	teaspoon salt
2	egg whites
	Pinch cream of tartar
1	teaspoon vanilla
1	cup chopped walnuts

1. Grease an 8-inch square pan; set aside. In a large saucepan, combine the sugars, water, corn syrup, and salt. Bring the mixture to a boil, stirring constantly. Continue to boil, without stirring, about 15 minutes or until syrup reaches 265°F on a candy thermometer (hard-ball stage).

2. Just before the sugar reaches temperature, whisk the egg whites and cream of tartar with an electric mixer until soft peaks form (tips curl). With the mixer on medium speed, pour the hot syrup slowly down the inside of the bowl, avoiding the whisk. Continue to beat until the mixture loses its gloss, about 10 minutes. Stir in the vanilla and nuts. Press the mixture into the prepared pan; smooth the top with a greased rubber scraper or spoon. Let divinity set before cutting into pieces.

makes about 25 pieces

Photo: Joseph Marini Sr. making candy in the original candy kitchen on the Santa Cruz Beach Boardwalk

"Talk about divine inspiration!" — JAMIE

Chocolate and Caramel Turtles

Our recipe for these chewy chocolates is simple to make—and even simpler to eat. And yes, they do look a little like turtles, if you use your imagination!

1	pound vanilla caramel candies
3	tablespoons unsalted butter
8	ounces salted pecans or cashews
1	12-ounce package semisweet chocolate chips

1. Grease 2 large cookie sheets; set aside. In a double boiler or a microwave set on low power, melt the caramels and butter, stirring frequently until smooth.

2. Arrange 36 groups of 3 nuts 2 inches apart on prepared cookie sheets (see photo, opposite). Spoon melted caramel by teaspoons on top of the nuts. Cool for 15 minutes.

3. In a double boiler or a microwave set on low power, melt the chocolate chips, stirring frequently until smooth. Spoon the melted chocolate by teaspoons over each caramel turtle. Spread the chocolate with a spatula. Let candies set at room temperature, or to speed up the setting process, refrigerate briefly.

makes 36 pieces

PHIL'S FISH MARKET

MOSS LANDING, CALIFORNIA

California isn't all sunbathing beauties, and the best catch isn't necessarily wearing a bikini; the West Coast bays bring in some of the country's freshest seafood. Moss Landing smells serious as you get close, and it is. It's an industrial fishery full of hardcore fishermen unloading boats; the only sunbathers we saw were a pack of sea lions, some weighing as much as 400 pounds. Right by the water we found Phil's Fish Market and Eatery, with a sign over the door that says, "Phil's still doing fish."

Behind the scenes, Phil DiGirolamo turns the pick of the catch into a classic San Francisco stew called cioppino. Before he opened the eatery, Phil demonstrated how to make the stew in an electric wok for his fish

market customers. It was such a hit, people started asking to take some home, and soon customers were bringing their own pots to fill. Word about the cioppino got around, and now customers enjoy the stew in the restaurant or by the pot to go. On holidays Phil has had up to 150 customers lined up outside with pots.

We helped toss sashimi-quality fish, crabs, scallops, squid, clams, mussels, and prawns into the stew pot under the supervision of Mr. Phil himself. In went pesto, a heady pinch of saffron ("the secret ingredient"), a tomato sauce flavored with cinnamon and brown sugar, Worcestershire, and some "good love." Out came a lunch so good it could almost give the gumbo we eat at Mama's table a run for the money.

Shrimp Gumbo

Full of bell pepper, onion, celery, thyme, and, most important, the deep, toasty flavor that you get from cooking flour, this is everything a good Cajun gumbo ought to be.

2 tablespoons vegetable oil
1 10-ounce package frozen
   sliced okra, thawed
1 medium onion, finely chopped
1 green bell pepper, finely chopped
1 stalk celery, finely chopped
1 clove garlic, minced
   Salt and freshly ground
   black pepper
2 tablespoons all-purpose flour
½ pound andouille sausage or
   kielbasa, halved lengthwise
   and sliced crosswise into
   ½-inch-thick pieces
2 cups canned chopped
   tomatoes, undrained
¼ teaspoon cayenne pepper
6 cups low-sodium chicken broth
2 sprigs fresh thyme
2 pounds medium shrimp,
   peeled and deveined
1 scallion, thinly sliced
1 tablespoon finely chopped
   fresh parsley
   Hot cooked rice

1. In a Dutch oven or soup pot, heat oil over medium heat. Add okra and cook for 15 to 20 minutes or until dry. Add onion, green pepper, celery, and garlic. Season with salt and pepper to taste. Increase heat to medium-high and saute about 5 minutes or until vegetables are soft.

2. Sprinkle the flour over the vegetables; cook and stir for 2 minutes. Add the sausage; cook about 5 minutes or until lightly browned, stirring occasionally. Stir in the undrained tomatoes and cayenne pepper. Stir in the broth and thyme sprigs, scraping up any brown bits from the bottom of the pan. Simmer, partially covered, for 1 hour, stirring occasionally.

3. Add shrimp and scallion. Season to taste with additional salt. Cook and stir about 3 minutes or until the shrimp are opaque. Discard the thyme sprigs. Stir in the parsley. Serve gumbo over rice.

makes 4 to 6 servings

The Deen Brothers' Cioppino

Wherever there is fresh seafood, there is usually a great recipe for seafood stew. We came up with this simplified version of cioppino after visiting Phil's Fish Market. Add some crusty bread and you'll be in for a real treat.

3	tablespoons olive oil
1	medium onion, finely chopped
1	stalk celery, finely chopped
4	garlic cloves, thinly sliced
½	cup dry white wine
4	cups canned chopped tomatoes, undrained
½	cup roasted red peppers, diced
1	teaspoon dried thyme
1	teaspoon dried oregano
¼	teaspoon red pepper flakes
	Salt and freshly ground black pepper
2	cups low-sodium chicken broth
1	cup bottled clam juice
1	pound firm white fish (such as cod, halibut, striped bass, or red snapper), cut into 1-inch pieces
1	pound medium shrimp, peeled and deveined
½	pound sea scallops or ½ pound crabmeat
24	small clams in the shell, scrubbed
1	to 2 tablespoons freshly squeezed lemon juice
¼	cup fresh Italian parsley leaves (optional)
	Crusty Italian bread

1. In a Dutch oven or soup pot, heat oil over medium heat. Add onion, celery, and garlic. Cook about 15 minutes or until vegetables are soft and beginning to brown. Add the wine; let simmer about 5 minutes or until most of the wine has evaporated.

2. Add the undrained tomatoes and the roasted red peppers. Add the thyme, oregano, and red pepper flakes. Season to taste with salt and pepper. Bring to a simmer. Add the broth; return to a simmer. Cook, partially covered, for 45 minutes, stirring occasionally. Add the clam juice and continue cooking, uncovered, for 5 minutes.

3. Stir in the fish pieces; cook for 5 minutes. Stir in the shrimp and scallops; cook for 5 minutes. Stir in the clams. Cook, stirring constantly, about 3 minutes or until the clams open. Discard any clams that don't open. Stir in lemon juice to taste. Ladle cioppino into bowls, sprinkle with fresh parsley leaves (if desired), and serve with crusty bread on the side.

makes 6 servings

PIKE PLACE FISH MARKET
SEATTLE, WASHINGTON

Folks stopped at Pike Place Fish Market to watch while Dan Bugge (with his red faux-hawk hairstyle) threw fish at us. At first we kept our eyes on the fish, but Dan is a seasoned professional who could throw a 20-pound salmon right between our heads from 20 feet away.

Dan knows fish, whether he's throwing them Seattle-style to the other fish guys or throwing them Spanish-style into a simmering pot of paella. In fact Dan's cooking is so good that he and his wife, Alisa, are opening a restaurant. We were lucky to catch him while he was still throwing fish.

Pike Place Market is known as "the Soul of Seattle," and its liveliest spot is Pike Place Fish Market. The guys there can work a crowd throwing their fish around, but beyond the show, they offer wonderful just-caught Pacific fish and seafood and sell complete paella kits to go with them.

We helped make the paella right there. The first step, gathering the ingredients, is the most important. We picked out beautiful Dungeness crabs, Manila clams, spot prawns, mussels, and a delicacy the fish guys call "butt cheeks." These firm, white pieces of fish are actually halibut cheeks. Cooked together with rice, tomatoes, thyme, coriander, red peppers, and two kinds of sausage, that pot of food was fit for two boys who grew up eating some of the best fish boils in the South.

Low-Country Boil

Our traditional boil, famous in the Low Country of Georgia and South Carolina, can be cooked indoors or out. The fun part is pouring it out on a picnic table covered in newspaper for an all-you-can-eat buffet.

1	gallon water
2	tablespoons crab boil or Old Bay seasoning
2	tablespoons salt
2	small cloves garlic, minced
12	small new potatoes, scrubbed
1½	pounds andouille or smoked sausage, halved lengthwise and sliced crosswise into ½-inch-thick pieces
6	ears corn, cleaned and each cut crosswise into 3 pieces
3	pounds medium shrimp

1. In a large stockpot, combine water, crab boil, salt, and garlic; bring to a boil. Add potatoes; boil for 15 to 20 minutes or until almost tender. Add the sausage; boil for 5 minutes. Add the corn; boil for 5 minutes. Add the shrimp; boil for 3 minutes more. Ladle into bowls or pour onto a newspaper-lined table outside to serve.

makes 6 servings

< Fried Halibut Sandwiches

We love fried fish sandwiches; these are inspired by the gorgeous halibut we saw in Seattle. If you plan on making this recipe in cold weather, turn on your kitchen exhaust fan before you start frying.

2	tablespoons mayonnaise
1	tablespoon Dijon mustard
1	tablespoon chopped fresh dill
2	8-ounce halibut fillets, skin removed
2	tablespoons all-purpose flour
½	teaspoon salt
	Freshly ground black pepper
1	tablespoon olive oil
2	kaiser or other large sandwich rolls, halved and toasted
1	tomato, sliced
1	red onion, thinly sliced

1. In a small bowl, whisk together the mayonnaise, mustard, and dill. Set aside.

2. Rinse fish and pat dry; set aside. In a shallow dish, stir together the flour, salt, and pepper to taste. Dip each fillet in the flour mixture to coat.

3. In a skillet, heat oil over medium-high heat. Cook the fish in the hot oil for 2 to 3 minutes per side or until golden.

4. Spread the dill mayonnaise evenly on the rolls. Place a fish fillet on each roll and top with tomato and onion slices.

makes 2 servings

< Easy Coleslaw

This salad gets better as it sits. Make it early in the morning for an afternoon barbecue.

4	cups (8 ounces) shredded cabbage or prepared coleslaw mix
4	scallions, trimmed and thinly sliced
½	teaspoon caraway seeds
¼	cup prepared coleslaw dressing

1. In a large bowl, combine all ingredients. Toss to coat.

makes 2 servings

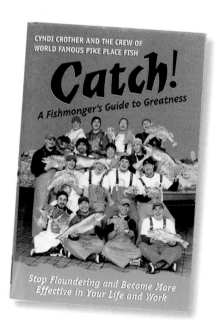

ALASKA SILK PIE
SEATTLE, WASHINGTON

Phyllis Buzzini was ready for us—she had already made her white- and dark-chocolate silk behind closed doors because she does not share her recipe for Alaska Silk Pie. Once we tasted that rich chocolate mousse, we could see why she wants to hold on to her invention.

The idea for Alaska Silk Pie came while Phyllis was running her first business, a wine bar in Alaska. The most popular dessert was a French silk pie, and she remembers how customers couldn't seem to get enough of it. That gave her the idea to try to replicate that pie and maybe even improve on it. As she puts it, since she didn't have much cooking experience, she didn't know her own limitations.

She knew right away when she got that incredible silky chocolate formula right, but Phyllis didn't stop there. She made a base of almonds, orange, spices, and caramel, then added six layers of alternating white- and dark-chocolate silk, each flavored with a different combo of grown-up flavors: espresso, cognac, orange liqueur, cinnamon, cloves, and orange. The final layer is topped with crunchy mocha beans. She ended up with a treat so beautiful and original, it caught on among folks in "the lower 48," as they say in Alaska. Phyllis was shipping so many pies out of Alaska, it just didn't make sense to stay there, so she moved to Seattle.

Alaska Silk Pies helped Phyllis make a new life for herself and her three lovely daughters. We didn't get her recipe, but we sure were glad to meet Phyllis and to hear her beautiful success story—especially over a silky-licious piece of that pie!

Alaskan Salmon Salad with Iceberg Lettuce

This salad tastes just like a lighter, crunchier salmon Big Mac®. Try it—you'll see!

RUSSIAN DRESSING:

2	tablespoons ketchup
2	tablespoons mayonnaise
1	tablespoon Dijon mustard
1	tablespoon finely chopped gherkins
1	teaspoon lemon juice

SALAD:

2	8-ounce salmon fillets*
	Salt and freshly ground black pepper
2	tablespoons unsalted butter, melted
2	tablespoons lemon juice
1	tablespoon chopped fresh dill
½	head iceberg lettuce, cut into wedges or shredded
½	red onion, thinly sliced

1. In a small bowl, whisk together all the dressing ingredients. Set aside.

2. For the salad, season each fillet with salt and pepper. In a microwave-safe baking dish, combine the butter and lemon juice. Place the fish in the dish, turning to coat. Sprinkle with fresh dill. Cover dish with plastic wrap and poke several holes in the plastic with a fork. Microwave on high (100% power) for 2 to 3 minutes or until the fish flakes easily with a fork. Once fish is cool enough to handle, remove any skin and flake the salmon into chunks.

3. Divide the lettuce and onion between two plates. Place salmon chunks on top of the lettuce. Drizzle the dressing over the salad.

*Use Alaskan salmon if you can find it.

makes 2 servings

< Chilly Banana Pudding

½ cup sugar
3 tablespoons cornstarch
2 cups whole milk
3 egg yolks
1 teaspoon vanilla
1 teaspoon rum (optional)
2 ripe bananas, sliced
   Coconut sorbet or vanilla
      ice cream

1. In a saucepan, whisk together sugar and cornstarch. Slowly add milk. Bring to a boil, whisking constantly. Reduce heat to medium. Cook 5 minutes or until thickened; stir constantly. Remove from heat.

2. Beat egg yolks until smooth. Whisking constantly, slowly add hot milk mixture (be careful not to curdle eggs). Return egg mixture to saucepan; cook over medium-low heat for 5 to 7 minutes or until thick, stirring constantly. Remove from heat; add vanilla and, if desired, rum.

3. Divide banana slices among four 12-ounce glasses. Spoon pudding over top. Chill for 2 hours or until set. Serve with sorbet.

makes 4 servings

Double-Chocolate Icebox Cake

2 cups heavy cream
5 tablespoons sugar
¼ cup unsweetened cocoa powder
1 teaspoon vanilla
1 9-ounce package chocolate
      wafer cookies
2 ounces bittersweet
      chocolate, shaved

1. Line an 8×4-inch loaf pan with plastic wrap, letting enough hang over the edges to cover the cake later. In a large bowl, stir together the cream, sugar, cocoa, and vanilla. Chill for 1 hour to let cocoa dissolve. Whip the chilled mixture until firm peaks form. Spoon two-thirds of mixture into prepared pan; spread evenly. Stand cookies on edge in the cream, making two lengthwise rows. Spread remaining mixture over cookies. Fold plastic wrap over top of cake; cover with foil. Refrigerate 6 hours or overnight.

2. Uncover cake, invert onto platter, and remove plastic wrap. Garnish cake with shaved chocolate.

makes 6 to 8 servings

MACRINA BAKERY AND CAFE
SEATTLE, WASHINGTON

Leslie Mackie's artisan breads and baked goods are famous well beyond Seattle. But she stays true to her location by using plenty of local sour cherries, which are one of Washington's most delicious products.

Dried cherries are ideal for baking because they have intense cherry flavor and just the right amount of sweetness. But when we went into Leslie's cozy, old-fashioned little bakery to learn about her Lemon Sour-Cherry Coffee Cake, a big bowl of fresh cherries was waiting for us (and we could not stop eating them).

While we were stealing cherries, Leslie showed us how she makes her coffee cake, mixing it gently by hand. She uses yogurt to keep it light, plumps dried cherries in a little warm water so they're nice and moist, and adds a very healthy amount of lemon zest for tang. Leslie bakes the cake in a fluted tube pan, drizzles it with lemon glaze, then scatters the top with more cherries and with crystallized flowers for a perfect presentation. Those flowers are a simple, absolutely beautiful way to dress up a cake—a trick we just might copy next time we're baking.

When it was done, that cake was a balanced mix of sweet and sour, with a tender texture that made us want more before we had finished our first slice. It's the kind of cake we could eat for breakfast, lunch, and dessert every day, and luckily, we had a whole beautiful cake in front of us. Sometimes life really is a bowl of cherries.

Apple-Bacon Corn Bread

In the South, when we make bread, it's usually corn bread. Here is one of our favorite recipes, loaded with yet another of Washington's famous products—sweet, juicy apples.

4	strips bacon
2	Granny Smith apples, peeled, cored, and finely chopped
1	cup all-purpose flour
¾	cup yellow cornmeal
3	tablespoons sugar
1½	teaspoons baking powder
½	teaspoon baking soda
½	teaspoon ground black pepper
¼	teaspoon salt
1½	cups buttermilk
2	eggs
5	tablespoons unsalted butter, melted

1. Preheat oven to 425°F. Butter a 9-inch square baking pan; set aside.

2. In a medium skillet, fry the bacon until crisp. Drain on a paper-towel-lined plate, then crumble the bacon into small pieces. Set aside.

3. Drain all but 1 tablespoon bacon drippings from the pan. Cook the apples in hot drippings over medium-high heat for 5 minutes, stirring frequently. Set aside.

4. In a large bowl, whisk together the flour, cornmeal, sugar, baking powder, baking soda, pepper, and salt. In a medium bowl, beat together the buttermilk, eggs, and butter. Fold the buttermilk mixture into the flour mixture. Fold in the bacon and apples. Pour the batter into the prepared pan.

5. Bake for 25 to 30 minutes or until golden and a knife inserted in the center comes out clean. Cool for 10 minutes before serving.

makes 8 servings

Cherry-Stuffed Pecan Streusel Coffee Cake

*Our coffee cake rivals Leslie's original with
a luscious cherry jam layer in the center.*

STREUSEL:

2¾	cups all-purpose flour
2	teaspoons ground cinnamon
1	cup packed brown sugar
½	teaspoon salt
1	cup (2 sticks) unsalted butter, softened and cubed

CAKE:

2½	cups all-purpose flour
2	teaspoons ground cinnamon
1	teaspoon baking powder
½	teaspoon baking soda
¼	teaspoon salt
¾	cup (1½ sticks) unsalted butter, softened
1¼	cups granulated sugar
3	eggs
1	teaspoon vanilla
1¼	cups sour cream
1	cup cherry jam
⅓	cup chopped pecans

1. Preheat oven to 350°F. Grease a 10-inch tube pan; set aside.

2. For the streusel, in a medium bowl, whisk together the 2¾ cups flour, 2 teaspoons cinnamon, the brown sugar, and ½ teaspoon salt. Use your fingers to cut in the cubed butter until the mixture forms medium-coarse crumbs. Set streusel aside.

3. For the cake, in a large bowl, whisk together the 2½ cups flour, 2 teaspoons cinnamon, the baking powder, baking soda, and ¼ teaspoon salt. In the bowl of an electric mixer, cream the ¾ cup butter and the granulated sugar until fluffy. Beat in the eggs, one at a time. Beat in the vanilla. Alternately beat in flour mixture and the sour cream.

4. Spoon half of the cake batter into the prepared pan, making sure to spread the batter to the edges of the pan. Top with half of the streusel. Evenly spoon the cherry jam over the streusel. Add the remaining cake batter, again spreading the batter to the edges of the pan. Stir the pecans into the remaining streusel; sprinkle the mixture on top of the batter. Bake for 1¼ to 1½ hours or until a long knife inserted into the cake comes out clean.

5. Cool the cake in the pan on a wire rack for 20 minutes. Run a knife along the inner and outer edges of the pan. Pulling the tube portion, lift the cake out of the pan. Slice and serve.

makes 12 servings

White Bean Soup

Leslie also presents specialty soups in homemade bread bowls for an outstanding lunch. Our version is quicker to make and no less fun to serve.

1	tablespoon olive oil
1	tablespoon unsalted butter
1	yellow onion, chopped
2	teaspoons chopped garlic
¼	cup tomato paste
2	15½-ounce cans white beans, drained
4	cups low-sodium chicken broth
	Salt and freshly ground black pepper
4	small round loaves bread (optional)
2	teaspoons chopped fresh parsley

1. In a soup pot, heat the oil and butter over medium heat. Add onion; saute for 3 to 5 minutes or until softened. Add the garlic; saute about 1 minute or until fragrant. Stir in the tomato paste. Add white beans and broth; bring to a boil.

2. Reduce heat and simmer for 20 minutes. Add salt and pepper to taste. Transfer the soup to a blender or food processor; puree until fairly smooth.

3. If desired, slice the top off each of the loaves and hollow out about 1½ cups of bread from each. (Save bread to make croutons or bread crumbs later.) Ladle the soup into the bread bowls and garnish with parsley.

makes 4 servings

"warms you up on a rainy Seattle afternoon"— BOBBY

The Midwest

WISCONSIN

On the shores of Lake Michigan, Milwaukee has it all: everything you want in a big city but with the charm and hospitality of a small town. They make Harley-Davidsons around here, and, more important, they make a lot of cheese—all the pretty cows we drove past were earning their keep. And from the great brewers of the beer world to the great Brewers of the baseball world, Milwaukee is the place to do what we like to do best: kick back and have fun. We did find time to do some serious eating and drinking while we were there. It's a tough job, but ...

ILLINOIS

In the early 20th century Chicago was right on the heels of New York in terms of its business and cultural activities, so it became known as the Second City. But this town is full of firsts—it boasts the first-ever commercial flight, grain reaper, softball game, elevated railway, winding watch, and Twinkie, among others. We agree that Chicago is a first-rate town, one proud of its distinctive neighborhoods, its architecture, Wrigley Field, and especially its people and their cooking. We tasted old-time recipes for everything from deep-dish pizza to buttery cookies, and we're happy to report that if they don't make 'em like they used to, it's because they're making 'em even better!

MISSOURI

St. Louis is in the heartland now, but when Lewis and Clark set out from there a century ago it was on the Western frontier, a place where immigrants came to find their futures. St. Louis honors its historic role as "Gateway to the West" with the iconic Gateway Arch, a great structure that towers over the city. History and tradition loom large here, as we found when we visited an old-world Italian deli and a German sausage maker, but innovation is just as important, even in small towns like Kimmswick, where we met a sweet lady in a ruffled blue apron who has built a bigger, better apple pie.

BEECHWOOD CHEESE COMPANY
BEECHWOOD, WISCONSIN

Among rolling green hills dotted with cows sits Beechwood Cheese Company, one of five factories still making their product by hand in what used to be the cheese capital of the world. As we quickly learned, these folks may use traditional methods, but they are far from old-fashioned.

When we met Mark and Kris Heise at the factory, they told us that to keep their business strong, they have added a big dose of innovation—and some very creative flavors—to their small-batch cheeses. Chipotle, mango-jalapeño, and salami cheese all sounded pretty good to us, but chicken soup flavor? We had to see it to believe it.

First we helped make a big vat of white Monterey Jack cheese, turning fresh local milk into cheese curds. Whoever kept working after they invented cheese curds was stronger than either of us—we could have stood there eating those squeaky-fresh curds till the cows came home. For her chicken soup flavor, Kris adds chicken soup concentrate and dried celery to the curds; then they are pressed into blocks and aged.

Mark has been making cheese for as long as he can remember, but it was only when he met Kris that the cheese at Beechwood got fancy. We were curious to try Kris' invention, and it turned out to be every bit as good as the combination of two great foods. Soup and cheese—talk about an inspired marriage! We came home with new appreciation for the power of cheese.

Classic Cheese Fondue

This is our take on the melty, cheesy Swiss recipe that America went crazy for in the '60s and '70s. We just love it on a chilly night.

1 clove garlic, halved
1½ cups dry white wine
8 ounces Gruyère cheese,
  shredded (about 2 cups)
8 ounces Emmentaler cheese,
  shredded (about 2 cups)
2 tablespoons cornstarch
  Ground white pepper
  Pinch nutmeg or cayenne pepper
1 baguette, torn into pieces
1 Granny Smith apple,
  cored and sliced

1. Rub the cut sides of the garlic over the inside bottom and sides of a medium saucepan. Add the wine and bring to a simmer; reduce heat to medium-low. In a large bowl, toss the cheeses with the cornstarch. Slowly add the cheese mixture to the simmering wine, stirring constantly (back and forth as well as around and around) about 4 minutes or until melted and smooth. Season to taste with white pepper and nutmeg.

2. Transfer the cheese mixture to a fondue pot. Serve with the bread and apple slices for dipping.

makes 4 servings

Pecan-Crusted Cranberry Cheese Balls

We make these around the holidays, and whenever we need a festive hors d'oeuvre. If you've got any young kitchen helpers around, enlist them to smoosh the cheese into balls.

8 ounces cheddar cheese,
  shredded (about 2 cups)
3 tablespoons cream cheese, softened
3 tablespoons dried
  sweetened cranberries
⅔ cup finely chopped pecans

1. In a bowl, mix together cheddar cheese, cream cheese, and cranberries. Form mixture into bite-size balls and roll in the pecans, pressing gently to help the nuts adhere. Refrigerate in an airtight container until ready to use. Let come to room temperature before serving.

makes about 30 balls

Baked Mac and Cheese

We enrich our mac and cheese with sour cream for an extra tangy layer of flavor. And we have never had any complaints—or leftovers!

2	cups uncooked elbow macaroni
8	ounces cheddar cheese, shredded (about 2 cups)
8	ounces American cheese, shredded (about 2 cups)
1	cup whole milk
½	cup sour cream
2	eggs
¼	cup unsalted butter, cut into pieces
1	teaspoon bottled hot pepper sauce or to taste (optional)
½	teaspoon salt

1. Preheat oven to 350°F. Grease a 9×13-inch baking dish; set aside. In saucepan, cook macaroni according to package directions; drain. Return macaroni to saucepan.

2. While the macaroni is hot, add the cheeses to the pan; stir well. Spread the macaroni mixture in the prepared baking dish. In a bowl, whisk together the milk, sour cream, eggs, butter, hot sauce, and salt. Pour the milk mixture over the macaroni.

3. Bake for 35 to 40 minutes or until golden brown and bubbling. Let stand for 10 minutes before serving.

makes 8 servings

VOTED #1 KRINGLE
4 Generations of Quality

BENDTSEN'S BAKERY
RACINE, WISCONSIN

We love pastry in all shapes and forms, so when we heard about the kringle, a sweet treat that resembles Danish pastry, we were prepared to love it sight unseen. We found out that a fellow named Bendt Bendtsen is one of the last people in Wisconsin making kringles by hand, so we went to pay our respects to his rich, flaky craft.

And it is a craft. Bendt's grandfather brought the recipe over from Denmark and passed it down through his family. It took Bendt about four years to learn how to make these round filled pastries, which start with a light, delicate yeast-leavened dough. It's the only job he's ever had, so he is certainly an expert.

Bendt made his work look easy, folding an enormous brick of butter into the dough to create 72 layers, then rolling it napkin-thin. He handed his masterpiece over to us to spread with raspberry jam; then he gave the pastry a few flips and had a perfect ring with the filling hidden inside.

Yeast in the dough causes the kringle to puff up as it bakes. We did not even let that pastry cool before we dug in; it was beyond wonderful, like squished raspberry pie. Knowing how much effort and expertise went into it just made it better. We could tell Bendt enjoyed watching us appreciate his hard work almost as much as we enjoyed eating it!

Cinnamon Bear Cub Claws

Made with purchased puff pastry, bear claws are similar to kringle in that they're tender, sweet, and made up of a million crunchy little layers. But bear claws are much easier to make—especially our speedy version.

ALMOND FILLING:

½	cup sliced almonds
¼	cup granulated sugar
6	tablespoons unsalted butter, softened
1	egg
½	teaspoon ground cinnamon
1	pound prepared puff pastry
⅓	cup golden raisins
1	egg plus 1 teaspoon water, whisked together
¼	cup turbinado (raw) sugar Sliced almonds

1. Preheat oven to 400°F. In a food processor, finely grind the almonds and sugar. Add the butter, egg, and cinnamon. Process until smooth. Set filling aside.

2. Roll out puff pastry to ¼-inch thickness. Using a 3-inch round cutter, cut out circles. Spoon 2 teaspoons almond filling in the center of each circle. Sprinkle each with raisins. Brush the edges of the circles with water. Fold the circles in half, pressing the edges to seal. Using a knife, cut four "claws" into the folded sides. Place pastries on a baking sheet.

3. Brush the tops of the pastries with the egg mixture. Sprinkle them with turbinado sugar and sliced almonds. Bake for 12 to 14 minutes or until golden.

makes 18 pastries

"unbearably sweet, crunchy, and delicious"—JAMIE

< Delicate Danish Butter Cookies

Growing up, we learned to appreciate the delicious taste that real butter gives to desserts. This recipe is our way of celebrating the wonderful flavor of our favorite shortening.

1	cup (2 sticks) unsalted butter, softened
¾	cup packed light brown sugar
1	egg yolk
½	teaspoon finely grated lemon zest
2	cups all-purpose flour
¼	teaspoon salt
¼	cup turbinado (raw) sugar

1. Cream the butter. Add the brown sugar; beat until fluffy. Beat in egg yolk and lemon zest. Add flour and salt; mix until just combined. Roll the dough into a log about 1½ inches in diameter (chill dough, if needed, for easier handling). Roll the log in the turbinado sugar. Wrap the log in plastic wrap and chill for 1 hour.

2. Preheat oven to 350°F. Slice dough log into ⅜-inch-thick rounds; place the rounds on 2 large baking sheets. Bake for 10 to 12 minutes or until light brown. Transfer cookies to a wire rack to cool.

makes 42 cookies

Kringle Bread Pudding

If you are less greedy than we are when it comes to eating kringle and you happen to have some leftovers, you can make this luscious bread pudding.

1	tablespoon unsalted butter, melted
1	1½-pound kringle, cubed (about 7 cups), or an equal amount Danish pastries
¼	cup bourbon
⅓	cup raisins
8	eggs
¾	cup packed light brown sugar
2	cups heavy cream
¾	cup whole milk
1	tablespoon vanilla
¼	teaspoon salt

1. Preheat oven to 300°F. Grease a 13×9-inch baking pan with butter and scatter kringle cubes over bottom of pan. In a saucepan, bring bourbon to a simmer; remove from heat. Stir in raisins; let steep for 10 minutes. In a large bowl, whisk together the eggs and sugar. Whisk in remaining ingredients, including the raisins and bourbon. Pour mixture over kringle in pan. Cover with plastic wrap and chill for 1 hour.

2. Bake the pudding, uncovered, about 1 hour or until just set. Let stand for 10 minutes before serving.

makes 12 servings

Ale

...tyle ale with subtle
...ss and soft finish

Silver
Medal
Winner

sprecherbrewery.com

Bavarian

*A dark Kulmbacher-style lager
with renowned smoothness and
distinctive flavors and aromas
of coffee, caramel and chocolate.*

sprecherbrewery.cc

Sprecher
Milwaukee's *Original* Micro-Brewery

E WEISS

*A coarse-filtered wheat ale fermented with a
German yeast culture for refreshingly
light spiciness and hints of citrus fruit.*

BRONZE MEDAL
WINNER!

South German-Style Hefeweizen
2005 LA County Fair

sprecherbrewery.com

Spre
Milwaukee's *Original* Micro-Br

Oktober

Best of Sh
Gold Medal W
2005 LA County F
Oktoberfest Catego

Gold Medal W
2004 Great American Bee
Oktoberfest Catego

recherbrewery.com

Sprecher
Milwaukee's *Original* Micro-Brewery

PA
a Pale Ale

*This traditional ale was
originally brewed in England for
the British troops stationed in India.
Double dry-hopped, it has intense hop
flavors and aromas delicately
balanced with a potent,
yet delicious malty sweetness.*

You won't be hoppy untill you try it!

sprecherbrewery.com

Sprec
Milwaukee's *Original* Micro-Brewer

*Generation
Porter*

1985

2005

Sprecher
Milwaukee's *Original* Micro-Brewery

2004 Great American Beer Festival®

Sprecher
Micro-

SPRECHER BREWING COMPANY
GLENDALE, WISCONSIN

Beer is definitely what made Milwaukee famous—but root beer helped, and down South, we just love a frosty mug of good root beer. We dropped in on brewmaster Randy Sprecher, who crafts both beer and root beer in his own brew house. When Randy started the business in 1985, people said, "You're crazy; how are you going to go up against the big guys?"

Maybe being crazy helped—Randy did remind us of a mad scientist mixing up a big, bubbling vat of his root beer, and certainly his secret recipe plays a big part in making Sprecher's the root beer folks request for their ice cream floats all over town. Randy uses

local honey, wintergreen, sarsaparilla, a host of botanicals, and vanilla in his brew, along with yucca extract and Lake Michigan water, which he claims makes everything brewed in Milwaukee that much better.

It is a superior product. Straight from the bottle or poured over a nice scoop of ice cream, that root beer has a supercreamy head and a flavor that certainly has the big guys beat. Randy doesn't limit himself to root beer though. Sprecher also produces craft beers, cream soda, cherry-cranberry red soda, orange soda, and ginger ale, not to mention some incredible root beer barbecue sauce, all made from proprietary "fire brewed" recipes.

Vanilla Chocolate Chip Root Beer Floats >

We decided that root beer floats are so good they deserve a little more respect. So we dress ours up and serve them as a dessert.

1	pint (2 cups) vanilla chocolate chip ice cream
1	liter (about 4 cups) root beer
	Whipped cream
	Shaved chocolate

1. Fill four glasses with scoops of ice cream. Pour the root beer over the ice cream. Top with whipped cream and shaved chocolate. Serve with straws and long spoons.

makes 4 servings

Ginger Ale-Glazed Ham

We grew up eating cola-glazed ham at parties, so it was only a matter of time before we started experimenting. This glaze has a great tangy-sweet flavor with a little bite from the mustard and cayenne.

½	boneless ham (3 to 4 pounds)
1	cup white wine
2½	tablespoons Dijon mustard
2	tablespoons molasses
	Pinch cayenne pepper
2	cups ginger ale
2	tablespoons honey

1. Preheat oven to 300°F. Place ham in a roasting pan. In a medium saucepan, combine the wine, mustard, molasses, and cayenne. Bring to a simmer and simmer for 5 minutes. Stir in the ginger ale. Pour the glaze over the ham. Bake for 1½ hours.

2. Increase oven temperature to 325°F. Bake for 1 hour more, basting the ham every 15 minutes. Brush the ham with the honey. Bake for 30 minutes more, basting every 15 minutes, until the ham is well glazed. Slice and serve.

makes 8 to 10 servings

LOU MALNATI'S PIZZERIA

LINCOLNWOOD, ILLINOIS

Until we visited Lou Malnati's Pizzeria, we had never tasted real deep-dish pizza, and we had absolutely no idea how to go about making one. Lou is the most famous name in pizza in Chicago, the capital of deep-dish, so we headed right for the flagship Malnati's restaurant in suburban Lincolnwood to get the story from Lou's oldest son, Marc Malnati.

Marc said that Lou began making pizza with his father in the 1940s and started his own pizzeria in 1971. Lou and his wife, Jean, grew the business and now have more than 20 family-owned Malnati's. So what's the secret to their success?

As with many family-owned businesses (our own included), it's all about taking pride in the details. For example, Marc said that the family goes to California every summer to oversee the canning of their sauce tomatoes. They make sure that within a six-hour window, perfectly ripe tomatoes go from vine to can. Then for the rest of the year, they simmer those juicy tomatoes into the rich, sunny-tasting sauce that is at the heart of Malnati's amazing pizza. Even the mozzarella cheese is specially made for the pizzeria at a small Wisconsin dairy. These guys may run a lot of pizzerias, but they still make every pie with the kind of care that made Lou famous.

And all their work pays off. The pizza is fresh and full of flavor, with a light, crunchy crust covered in layers of melting cheese, that incredible sauce, and savory, meaty pork sausage. Malnati's pizza is knife and fork food, and every slice offers a big, satisfying taste that is authentic Chicago.

The Deen Brothers' Deep-Dish Pizza >

Once we tasted how good authentic deep-dish pizza is, we knew we'd want to make our own so we could enjoy it again at home. And you can bet we did!

1   tablespoon olive oil
1   1-pound ball frozen pizza
      dough, thawed
      Large pinch salt
1   pound mozzarella cheese,
      shredded (about 4 cups)
1   cup tomato-basil pasta sauce
1   teaspoon dried oregano

1. Preheat oven to 500°F. Brush a 10-inch round cake pan with 2 teaspoons of the oil. Roll the dough into a 14-inch circle. Transfer the dough to the prepared pan, pushing it up the side and over the edge of the pan. Pinch the dough over the edge of the pan to seal it there. Brush the dough with the remaining 1 teaspoon oil and sprinkle with salt. Prick the dough all over with a fork. Bake about 10 minutes or until set. Remove from oven. Reduce oven temperature to 400°F.

2. Spread half of the cheese over the pizza dough. Spoon the tomato sauce over the cheese and top with the remaining cheese. Sprinkle the oregano evenly over the cheese. Bake for 10 to 15 minutes or until the crust is golden and the cheese is bubbling. Let stand a few minutes before slicing.

makes 4 servings

Goldbrick Sundaes

You probably have your own favorite ways of enjoying a bowl of ice cream. But once you try ours, which is based on a Chicago specialty, you just might have a new one.

1   cup milk chocolate chips
1   1.4-ounce chocolate-covered
      English toffee bar, crushed
⅓   cup chopped pecans
1   pint (2 cups) vanilla ice cream

1. In a double boiler or a microwave set on low power, melt the chocolate, stirring frequently. Fold in toffee bar and pecans. Serve sauce over ice cream.

makes 4 servings

KIM & SCOTT'S GOURMET PRETZELS
CHICAGO, ILLINOIS

"We dreamt of making pretzels and creating a life where we could work together—it's all twisted together," says Kim Holstein. Her husband, Scott, agrees that their business is a dream come true. And as soon as we tried this couple's unique stuffed pretzels, we were convinced of their saying: Taste the love … love the taste!

The Holsteins' great pretzels weren't born in a day though—the couple studied pretzel making with experts before they developed their own recipes in the kitchen of Kim's studio. In an inspired moment of pretzel logic, they took some of their pretzel dough and stuffed it to create an incredibly soft bread treat all twisted up with favorite American flavors like pizza, grilled cheese, berry cobbler, and apple pie. Kim and Scott started selling their products on the Home Shopping Network, and soon stores all over the country were carrying them. They opened a bakery to house their growing business.

These folks not only sell pretzels but want to bring everyone in on their passion. At their Twisted Cafe, kids can twist, top, and decorate their own pretzels and eat pretzel sandwiches. But after some serious taste testing, we have concluded that these treats aren't just child's play. Whether it's sweet chocolate pudding or savory spinach and feta that you crave, Scott and Kim have the answer, twisted up in a pretzel.

< Cheesy Pretzel Dipping Sauce

We serve this cheesy dipping sauce with pretzel sticks, but it's also great on everything from broccoli to tortilla chips. We've even been known to just eat it with a spoon.

½ cup milk
2 tablespoons unsalted butter
8 ounces sharp cheddar cheese, shredded (about 2 cups)
4 ounces cream cheese, softened
¼ cup sour cream
1 teaspoon prepared deli-style mustard
⅛ teaspoon bottled hot pepper sauce or more to taste
Salt and freshly ground black pepper
Assorted pretzels, for dipping

1. In a large saucepan, bring the milk and butter to a boil; reduce heat. Add cheddar cheese; whisk until smooth. Remove from heat. Add cream cheese, sour cream, mustard, and hot sauce; whisk until smooth. Season to taste with salt and pepper. Transfer sauce to serving dish. Serve sauce warm with pretzels. If the sauce starts to cool and firm up, heat it in the microwave on low power, stirring frequently.

makes 2 cups

Turkey and Cranberry Mayo Pretzel Sandwiches

We were so inspired by the idea of pretzel sandwiches, we took the idea and ran with it. This Thanksgiving-style sandwich, with a hint of cilantro, is one of our best combos.

⅓ cup mayonnaise
⅓ cup chopped fresh cilantro leaves
¼ cup canned whole-berry cranberry sauce
6 frozen pretzels, thawed, split, and toasted
¾ pound sliced turkey breast
1½ cups baby arugula or spring salad mix

1. In a small bowl, whisk together the mayonnaise, cilantro, and cranberry sauce. Spread the cut side of each pretzel half with some mayonnaise mixture. Top 6 pretzel halves evenly with the turkey and arugula. Top with remaining pretzel halves.

makes 6 servings

DESSE
CATER
SolomonsCookies.com G

E CATER!

$4.50 *per person*

els, Muffins, Schneckin, Croissants

$4.50 *per person*

es, Mango, Pineapple,
lueberries

$5.75 *per person*

ast Beef, Turkey, Tuna on White,
ye Bread, lettuce, tomato, cheese,
er person)

$3.50 *per person*

CKEN   +$1.00 *per person*

prese, Cornucopia $4.25 *per person*

$2.85 *per person*

wnies, Bars, & Cookies

Solomon's
KITCHEN & GIFTS

SOLOMON'S GOURMET COOKIES
CHICAGO, ILLINOIS

We knew the moment we met them that Adam and Jason Tenenbaum (who were sporting classic, Chicago-style fedoras like their grandfather used to wear) were a couple guys with a healthy respect for tradition. In fact Jason and Adam are so dedicated to their family traditions that after earning a Ph.D. and a law degree, respectively, they decided to turn back to the time-honored baking traditions of their grandmother, Frieda.

Frieda met Aaron Solomon in 1943, just before he went to serve in World War II, but she wouldn't marry him until he came back. She did, however, send him sweet reminders of her promise in the form of buttery homemade cookies—chocolate chip, jam thumbprints, and shortbread bars.

When Aaron returned they married, and Frieda kept baking. She had a list of

55 people to whom she sent her cookies, and nothing could convince her to make the list any longer. When her daughters, Sandra and Lynn, took over the old recipes, they opened Frieda's famous cookie list to the world by going into business. Third-generation Adam and Jason grew up on those cookies ("cookie" was Jason's first word), so it's no surprise that they have returned to their roots.

Frieda's recipes rely on starting from scratch, and her grandsons aren't cutting any corners—in fact they've added some corners by turning some of their grandmother's cookies into bars, which ship well, keep well, and taste incredible. From their fudgy chocolate-mint brownies to their chewy butterscotch, chocolate, and pecan-topped turtle bars, you can taste the heritage in every bite of these old-fashioned treats.

Chocolate-Peanut Butter Chippers

Thanks to our mom, we were lucky enough to grow up with a tradition of homemade cookies like this chocolate chip version.

2½	cups all-purpose flour
1	teaspoon baking soda
¼	teaspoon salt
1¼	cups smooth or crunchy peanut butter
1	cup (2 sticks) unsalted butter, softened
1½	cups packed light brown sugar
⅔	cup granulated sugar
2	large eggs
1	tablespoon light corn syrup
2	teaspoons vanilla
1	10-ounce bag milk or semisweet chocolate chips
½	cup chopped salted peanuts

1. Preheat oven to 350°F. Grease 2 large baking sheets; set aside.

2. In a large bowl, whisk together the flour, baking soda, and salt; set aside. In the bowl of an electric mixer, cream together the peanut butter, butter, and sugars until fluffy. Add the eggs, one at a time, beating after each addition. Beat in the corn syrup and vanilla. Slowly add the flour mixture; mix until fully combined. Fold in the chocolate chips and peanuts.

3. Drop the cookie dough by heaping teaspoons 2 inches apart onto the prepared baking sheets. Bake for 12 to 14 minutes or until golden brown around the edges. Transfer cookies to a wire rack to cool.

makes about 54 cookies

"Got cookies? Just add milk!"— BOBBY

Many Jam Thumbprints

If you use different-color jams, these look really festive and perfect for the holidays.

1½	cups all-purpose flour
¾	cup ground pecans
1	teaspoon baking powder
⅛	teaspoon salt
¾	cup (1½ sticks) unsalted butter, softened
¾	cup granulated sugar
1	egg
1	teaspoon vanilla
1½	cups finely chopped pecans
½	cup fruit jam (such as raspberry, strawberry, apricot, orange marmalade, or a variety)

1. Preheat oven to 375°F. Grease 2 large baking sheets; set aside.

2. In a large bowl, whisk together the flour, ground pecans, baking powder, and salt; set aside. In the bowl of an electric mixer, cream together the butter and sugar until fluffy. Beat in the egg and vanilla. Slowly add the flour mixture; mix until fully combined.

3. Roll the dough into 1-inch balls. Roll balls in the chopped pecans. Place the balls 2 inches apart on the prepared baking sheets. Using your finger, make a deep (not wide) indentation in the cookie and fill each depression with jam. Bake for 12 to 14 minutes or until light golden brown. Transfer cookies to a wire rack to cool.

makes about 42 cookies

"Now we're jammin'!"—JAMIE

SWISS MEATS
HERMANN, MISSOURI

Sausage is so simple, so full of flavor—it's about the tastiest food we know. Now we know what makes it so good.

We visited Hermann, Missouri, where the Sloan family makes 40 different kinds of bratwurst, from apple-cinnamon to garlic-butter. They originally made their German-style sausages in Swiss, Missouri, hence the name of their company, but as business grew they moved. It still looks like a rural farmhouse operation, but when you step inside, you know you're onto something big. Bill Sloan (also known as the Sausage King) and his four daughters and one son have amassed many awards for their excellent smoked meats and sausages. They are some of the best "bratologists" in the country, and we were eager to learn from the best.

Bill and his son, Mike, were happy to let us help. First we ground fresh pork (they have a slaughterhouse onsite, but we skipped that step!); then we hand-mixed pounds and pounds of the meat with cheese, mushrooms, and spices for the mushroom-Swiss brat.

Then the Sausage King took over, cranking an antique sausage stuffer with one hand while holding the end of a casing with the other to create a long, perfect sausage. He twisted that sausage into a figure eight to form the brats (brat means "link" in German). The Sloans smoke their sausages over hickory, cherry, apple, or maple wood for about six hours, which gives them a wonderful fresh, meaty flavor and a gentle, smoky taste. But take it from us, it is much easier to eat sausage than to make it.

Bratwurst and Granny Smith Apple Salad

This recipe was inspired by the flavors of Germany. Sour cream, sausage, and pickles make this our kind of salad.

1	pound bratwurst
1	Granny Smith apple, peeled, cored, and grated
¾	cup sour cream
3	tablespoons prepared horseradish
1	teaspoon lemon juice
	Pinch salt
¼	cup coarsely chopped fresh parsley
¼	cup chopped sweet or sour pickle (optional)

1. Preheat broiler. Place bratwurst on a baking sheet or broiler pan. Broil 4 to 5 inches from heat for 5 to 7 minutes or until heated through, turning bratwurst once. When cool enough to handle, quarter bratwurst lengthwise, then cut crosswise into 1-inch pieces.

2. In a medium bowl, stir together the apple, sour cream, horseradish, lemon juice, and salt. Add the bratwurst, parsley, and pickle (if using); stir to combine. Serve cold or at room temperature.

makes 6 to 8 servings

Brat and Bean Casserole

We love sausage in every form, including franks 'n' beans. We put some crispy crumbs on top to make these extra special.

1	tablespoon olive oil
1	yellow onion, thinly sliced
1	pound bratwurst, cut into fat slices
2	16-ounce cans baked beans
½	cup bread crumbs

1. Preheat oven to 400°F. In a 4-quart ovenproof pot or Dutch oven, heat the oil over medium-high heat. Add the onion; saute for 7 to 10 minutes or until golden. Add bratwurst; saute for 5 to 7 minutes or until brown.

2. Add baked beans and bring to a simmer. Top with the bread crumbs. Bake, uncovered, about 40 minutes or until bubbly and golden.

makes 4 to 6 servings

Midwestern-Style Beer Brats

When we learned about the way they cook sausages in beer in the Midwest, we were inspired. We went right home and cooked up a pot ourselves.

6   bratwurst
6   cups lager beer
2   large onions, sliced
1   tablespoon olive oil
2   red or green bell peppers,
        cored and sliced
      Salt and freshly ground
        black pepper
6   bratwurst buns or hoagie
        rolls, split lengthwise
      Mustard

1. Prick the bratwurst all over with a fork. In a medium pot, combine the bratwurst, beer, and half the onions. Bring to a simmer over medium-high heat. Simmer about 15 minutes or until bratwurst are firm and cooked through. Transfer the bratwurst to a plate. Reserve some of the cooking liquid.

2. Meanwhile, in a large skillet, heat the oil over medium-high heat. Add the remaining onions and the bell peppers. Cook about 15 minutes or until very soft, tossing occasionally. Add the bratwurst to the skillet in the last 5 minutes of cooking to lightly brown. If the vegetables begin to get too dark, add a few tablespoons of the bratwurst cooking liquid. Season to taste with salt and black pepper.

3. To serve, spread each bun with mustard. Fill each bun with a brat. Top with sauteed peppers and onions.

makes 6 servings

VOLPI
ITALIAN FOODS
ST. LOUIS, MISSOURI

We love authentic Italian prosciutto so much, so we were thrilled that a family in St. Louis was going to show us how to make it. To learn about this delicious subject, we drove by bocce gardens and trattorias in St. Louis' little Italy (a neighborhood called The Hill) to meet up with Armando and Lorenza Pasetti, the second- and third-generation owners of Volpi's deli. They make all kinds of cured, dried Italian meats the old-fashioned way, and their shop smells like a pork paradise. On the wall is a picture of Mr. Volpi making prosciutto with a cigar hanging out of his mouth. The recipes are the same as they were 100 years ago, but you can bet no one is smoking around that ham nowadays!

In fact prosciutto is unsmoked, which is the main difference between the Italian version and good old Southern ham. Both begin with a fresh ham that is coated with sea salt, then hung to cure for three weeks. Next they are rinsed, but while a Virginia ham is smoked to dry it out, the Italian method relies on time to do the same thing. Eight months later, the meaty, full-flavored dry ham is intensely tasty, no matter how you slice it (though thinner is better).

Lorenza showed us some interesting ways to enjoy prosciutto: with fresh mozzarella, figs, asparagus, breadsticks—and after extensive tasting, we decided our favorite was all of them!

Prosciutto and Melon Salad >

The folks at Volpi's make a superbly simple roll-up of fresh mozzarella, fresh basil, and their amazing prosciutto, which they call rottola. It inspired us to see how we could dress up Italian meats for a party.

1	large cantaloupe, halved lengthwise, seeds removed
8	thin slices prosciutto, torn into strips
2	tablespoons Italian (sweet) vermouth or cream sherry
	Fresh mint leaves for garnish

1. Cut the melon into wedges, then carve away the rind.

2. Arrange the melon wedges on a platter. Lay prosciutto strips over melon wedges. Drizzle vermouth over the prosciutto and garnish with mint leaves. Serve immediately.

makes 4 servings

Prosciutto-Wrapped Cheese Straws

Prosciutto is a great complement to sweet and fresh flavors. A simple, beautiful presentation like this will be a hit at your next gathering.

12	cheese straws or breadsticks (about 4 ounces)
½	cup black olive tapenade or paste
12	thin slices prosciutto

1. Using your fingers or a butter knife, spread about 2 teaspoons tapenade on each cheese straw, leaving an inch at the bottom of the straw to act as a handle. Starting at the top of each straw, spiral a slice of prosciutto around the straw, stopping where the tapenade stops. Serve immediately.

makes 12 pieces

Salami, Mozzarella, and Basil-Tomato Skewers

These skewers make nice appetizers for a summer barbecue or potluck.
You can also skip the grilling and serve them at room temperature.

12   bamboo skewers
12   ounces salami, cut into 1-inch cubes
12   ounces smoked mozzarella,
      cut into 1-inch cubes
24   cherry tomatoes
24   basil leaves
      Olive oil
      Freshly cracked black pepper

1. Soak skewers in water for 30 minutes. Preheat broiler or prepare grill.

2. On each skewer, thread a cube of salami, a cube of mozzarella, and a basil-wrapped cherry tomato. Repeat with additional salami, mozzarella, tomato, and basil.

3. Place the skewers on a baking sheet. Broil 4 to 5 inches from heat about 1 minute or until just warm. (If grilling, place them on the grill over low heat, or as the coals are burning down, for 1 to 2 minutes, turning once.) Watch skewers carefully so that the cheese softens a little but does not melt.

4. Arrange skewers on a serving platter. Drizzle with oil and sprinkle with cracked pepper. Serve warm.

makes 6 servings

by Heather Berry

The Blue Owl

Southern hospitality in Kimmswick

At 2 a.m. most people are tucked into their beds, dreaming sweet dreams. But in the Mississippi River town of Kimmswick, 25 minutes south of St. Louis, there's one business getting an early start.

Bakers at The Blue Owl Restaurant and Bakery begin making their popular pastries and desserts in the middle of the night. That's because they need to have the bakery cases filled by 10 a.m. before the restaurant opens for business.

When you walk into this charming restaurant it's almost like visiting friends.

"We want to welcome customers into The Blue Owl as we would company into our homes," says Mary Hostetter, 51, owner of the restaurant.

The warmth and hospitality felt at this quaint establishment isn't by accident. Mary hails from Texas where southern hospitality and entertaining almost seems to be bred into folks.

"My grandma was a baker from Germany and she lived just around the corner from us in Galveston, so my mother and I've always loved baking and cooking," says Mary.

After high school she married and started a family. Soon her husband's job transfer brought them to St. Louis.

It was her faith and the strength of family and new friends which pulled Mary through the dark hours that came next, as her marriage ended in divorce.

With two young girls, no job and living far away from Texas, Mary didn't have a clue what she was going to do. But being the positive person she is, she decided to make lemonade out of the lemons life handed her.

"I decided to start baking cookies and pastries out of my home to sell at craft shows," she says. "It was something I knew I could do."

She lined silver trays with delicacies such as baklava, Russian tea cakes, pecan tartlets and Hungarian butterhorns and sold them for 50 cents each or three for a dollar. Pretty soon people were ordering platters of goodies and requesting pies and cakes.

A year later, during the 1984 holiday season, Mary had orders for more than 30,000 cookies. "The phone rang off the wall," she says.

Mary had to work 21 hours a day, seven days a week to get those orders completed. During the day,

Mary Hostetter, owner of The Blue Owl Restaurant and Bakery, proudly displays one of her bakery's fine caramel-apple pecan pies, one of more than 40 pies she offers.

The Blue Owl Restaurant & Bakery

Specialties: Tropical turkey salad, homemade chicken and dumplings, meatloaf, Southern fried chicken or chicken-fried steak with real milk gravy. For dessert, try the absolutely perfect strawberry-rhubarb pie, death-by-chocolate cake or a warm slice of the caramel-apple pecan pie.

Price: Breakfast $3.95 - $8.95 and lunch $3.95 - $11.95. A slice of homemade pie, cake or cheesecake runs $4.95 to $5.95. Kids menu, $3.95.

Hours: Tuesday through Friday from 10 a.m. to 3 p.m.; Saturday and Sunday from 10 a.m. to 5 p.m. Open year-round. Reservations recommended — or arrive early to get on the waiting list!

Credit cards: Visa, Mastercard, Discover and American Express accepted. Debit cards and checks also accepted. The only ATM in town is on site.

Kimmswick•

Directions: Take I-55 south of St. Louis to exit 186, east to Hwy. 61-67, south to Hwy K.

bake until the wee hours of the morning.

After surviving the Christmas deluge, Mary had to rethink her plan. She attended a class about starting small businesses and soon began searching for a place.

Her path crossed with Lucianna Ross, a former resident and visionary for much of what Kimmswick today. Lucianna had faith that Mary's plan would work and helped her start a restaurant and bakery.

That was 19 years ago. Mary began with five employees and now has up to 95 at times. What was once a quaint little blue and white two-bedroom house which held 5 seats for diners has been expanded to serve 225. According to Mary, nothing for 500 to 600 people to served lunch on weekdays, with weekends bringing anywhere from 700 to 900 diners to their doors.

Customers can enjoy their home cooked meals in rooms such as The Owl's Nest, the Texas Tea Room or Lucianna's Tea Room. They can also sit on the large covered deck, designed like a southern-style veranda, and listen to a dulcimer player over lunch. In the winter, the deck is enclosed and heated so its charm can be enjoyed all year long.

Every diner can find something to eat here, but Mary warns that this isn't a place for the diet conscious.

"When people come here, they're not worried about calories, they want the real thing."

While there you might want to try the popular tossed strawberry salad and a bowl of homemade soup or white chili. Specialty entrees include tropical turkey salad, baked chicken salad pie, rich quiches (made with whipping cream) or the special of the day, which can range from chicken-fried steak with real country gravy to homemade chicken and dumplings.

As you're relishing your lunch, keep the menu and try to figure out which of the more than 100 desserts you'd like to order. Actually you'll probably be so full from lunch you'll have to have dessert boxed up to eat later.

Before you leave, stop by the bakery and buy a meringue pie (with meringue standing an easy inches tall) or maybe a 6-pound, homemade German chocolate cheesecake or towering levee-high apple pie, made with 18 apples in every pie. Chocolate lovers might grab some death-by-chocolate cake to go — but don't forget the milk.

Mary credits her staff with much of The Blue Owl's success.

THE BLUE OWL
KIMMSWICK, MISSOURI

Mary Hostetter's story reminded us of Mama's: She turned to cooking after her divorce to help care for her two daughters, Kim and Kelly, and like Mama, she ended up cooking for more people than she'd ever dreamed. Before long, Ms. Mary had started the Blue Owl Restaurant and Bakery, where the waitresses wear floor-length, ruffled blue dresses and serve old-fashioned country-style food and some of the best homemade pies, cakes, cheesecakes, pastries, cookies, and candies.

But Ms. Mary didn't stop with a successful restaurant and bakery. After a flood nearly wiped out the town of Kimmswick in 1993, she decided to commemorate the levee that saved the town with her Levee-High Apple Pie. This 16-pound pie contains 18 apples, all stacked up in a regular old pie plate—we had to come take a look.

Nearly as big as Bobby's head, the pie is a feat of engineering—it isn't made; it's built. Ms. Mary peels and slices the apples, tosses them with cinnamon and sugar, and lays them one by one into a dome-shape bowl, packing them down as she goes. Then she inverts the bowl over the bottom piecrust in one quick swoop so the apples stay piled up when she removes the bowl. She drapes a top crust over them, crimps the edges, bakes, and ends up with the world's tallest apple pie.

But Ms. Mary doesn't stop there. She coats that pie with a warm caramel-pecan topping and serves it with a big scoop of vanilla ice cream. Fresh apple flavor, a rich crust, and nutty caramel—now that's one heck of a pie!

Boy Scout Baked Apples

Bobby learned how to make these apples when he was a Boy Scout, and he's been making them ever since. Serve them with pork chops or roasted pork.

4	apples, cored with bottoms left intact
4	tablespoons packed dark brown sugar
4	teaspoons unsalted butter
4	cinnamon sticks
8	whole cloves

1. Preheat oven to 375°F. Put 1 tablespoon brown sugar in the center of each apple; top each with 1 teaspoon butter. Insert a cinnamon stick into the brown sugar-filled center and stick 2 cloves into the sides of each apple.

2. Wrap apples individually with foil and place in a small roasting pan. Bake about 30 minutes or until just tender.

makes 4 servings

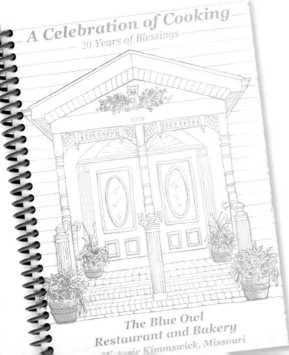

A Celebration of Cooking
20 Years of Blessings

The Blue Owl
Restaurant and Bakery
Historic Kimmswick, Missouri

Caramel Apple-Nut Crumb Pie

We had so much fun covering the Levee-High Apple Pie with caramel and nuts that we adapted the approach to our own pie recipe, which we make on a slightly less grand scale than the original.

FILLING:

½	cup sour cream
¾	cup warm dulce de leche or caramel sauce plus additional for drizzling
1	egg plus 1 egg yolk
¼	cup granulated sugar
2	tablespoons all-purpose flour
1	teaspoon vanilla
1	teaspoon freshly squeezed lemon juice
½	teaspoon ground cinnamon
¼	teaspoon ground nutmeg
¼	teaspoon salt
4	Granny Smith apples, peeled, cored, and thinly sliced
1	prepared 9-inch graham cracker crust*

TOPPING:

½	cup (1 stick) cold unsalted butter, cut into small pieces
½	cup packed light brown sugar
1	cup all-purpose flour
¼	teaspoon ground nutmeg
⅓	cup finely chopped walnuts or pecans

1. Preheat oven to 400°F. Whisk together the sour cream, ½ cup dulce de leche, and remaining filling ingredients except the apples. Fold in the apples. Spread the remaining ¼ cup dulce de leche on the bottom of the unbaked crust. Pour the apple mixture into piecrust. Bake for 30 minutes.

2. Meanwhile, in the bowl of an electric mixer, beat the butter, brown sugar, 1 cup flour, and ¼ teaspoon nutmeg on low speed until the flour is moistened but still crumbly. (Do not overmix.) With a fork, gently fold the chopped walnuts into the topping mixture.

3. Sprinkle the partially baked pie with the topping. Return the pie to the oven. Bake about 30 minutes more or until the top is golden brown. Drizzle the pie with additional dulce de leche. Let pie cool completely on a wire rack before slicing.

*The piecrust will be very full. Use a deep pie plate.

makes 8 servings

The East

NEW YORK—OUR FIRST VISIT

We knew we were in New York City because suddenly everything sped up. Yellow cabs went by so fast they blurred together, and we were in sensory overload. But we stayed focused on what we came for: old-school Italian food with big-city attitude. And we weren't disappointed—the city that never sleeps loves to eat. New York may be a fast town, but it's full of folks who take time to do things the old-fashioned way, making sausage, cheese, pastry, and bread from time-tested recipes brought over from Italy. Touring the great Italian eats of New York is like taking a history lesson; we learned about how immigrants came here generations ago, used what they knew, and worked with their families to achieve the American dream, New York-style.

NEW YORK—OUR SECOND VISIT

We didn't see nearly enough of the incredible New York City food scene on our first visit, so we came back for seconds and got a taste of the hot, sticky weather and brutal traffic that New Yorkers always complain about. But like them, we didn't let that stop us from running all over town, eating some of the most exciting, fun food we had ever had. At the end of the day, we were still hungry for more—there's just so much going on here—but you know, when you get to taste three cuisines in two boroughs in one day, you can't complain!

MAINE

Land of bean suppers, lobstermen, and pie-eating contests, Maine is full of opportunities for a couple of big eaters, and we wanted to try everything from chowder to biscuits and back again. Along the way, we found out that tradition doesn't rule here as much as we thought. These days Mainers are mixing up all kinds of tasty eats—we even found a place that makes lobster-flavored ice cream.

MARYLAND AND VIRGINIA

No road trip in America is complete without a stop in our nation's beautiful capital. Washington, D.C., is an all-American town with plenty of fine home cooking to be had. First we found some fittingly old-fashioned American fruit pie. Then we had crab cakes in mind, and we got our fill of the best, right where our country's politicians get theirs. But our last stop was the most surprising: We tasted cinnamon buns that were not only as good as any we've ever had but also much more healthy. That's American innovation for you—God bless America.

MIKE'S DELI

BRONX, NYC

We'd heard that Arthur Avenue, in the Bronx, is the spot for authentic Italian food stores, but we weren't prepared for what we found. In an indoor marketplace, we found a store that sells hand-rolled cigars, a butcher shop where rabbits and goats are displayed in the windows, and Mike's Deli, where a 250-pound provolone cheese hangs under the awnings. DeNiro and Pacino reportedly both shop here, but the real characters are the owners, Mike Greco and his son David. These guys are unbelievably nice—we immediately felt like their best friends. They poured some homemade moonshine and were making fun of our Southern accents inside of 10 minutes.

Our taste buds were in overdrive the whole time we were there, savoring aged Parmesan cheese, olives, prosciutto, fresh bread, and olive oil. Behind the counter, in about a foot of space, Mike has been making fresh mozzarella since 1947. "You have to make love to the cheese," he said, as David showed us how to break up the cheese curds, mix them with the "secret ingredient" (Bronx tap water), then pull them into milky, perfect white balls. David uses this mozzarella, along with homemade dough, potatoes, ham, onions, and peppers, to make the stuffed bread they call the Greco. The filling cooks and melts together as the bread bakes, and the result is light and looks fantastic.

Southern Stuffed Loaf

Our Southern take on classic Italian-American stuffed bread features the great flavors of mozzarella, roasted peppers, and pesto, all sandwiched into a tangy sourdough loaf.

1	1-pound round loaf sourdough bread
12	ounces fresh mozzarella, cut into cubes (about 3 cups)
1	cup coarsely chopped roasted red peppers
½	cup pine nuts, toasted and coarsely chopped
2	tablespoons pesto

1. Preheat the oven to 400°F. Cut the top third off the loaf of bread and scoop out 2 cups of bread from the bottom section. (Save scooped-out bread to make croutons or bread crumbs later.) Put the two pieces of bread on a baking sheet, cut sides up. Bake about 5 minutes or until lightly toasted.

2. In a large bowl, toss together the mozzarella, roasted peppers, and pine nuts. When bread is toasted, brush cut sides with pesto and spoon the mozzarella mixture into the bottom section. Put the top section on and wrap the whole loaf with foil. Bake wrapped loaf about 30 minutes or until warmed through. Unwrap and cut loaf into 4 to 6 wedges; serve immediately.

makes 4 to 6 servings

"This sandwich has got the right stuff." — BOBBY

< Prosciutto, Carpaccio-Style

We love all things pork, including thin-sliced Italian prosciutto. This recipe is our go-to lunch on a hot day.

8	ounces sliced prosciutto
3	ounces baby arugula
2	tablespoons extra virgin olive oil
1½	teaspoons red wine vinegar
	Salt and freshly ground black pepper
4	large plum tomatoes, cored, seeded, and chopped

1. Divide the prosciutto among 4 plates. Top each with an equal amount of arugula and drizzle each with ½ teaspoon of the oil.

2. In a small bowl, whisk together the remaining oil, the vinegar, and salt and pepper to taste. Add the tomatoes; toss to coat. Spoon the tomato salad onto the center of each plate.

makes 4 servings

Chopped Salad, Arthur Avenue-Style

Man cannot live on fried chicken and cream pie alone. Sometimes we crave a good salad, and this tangy, crunchy recipe has enough cheese and meat to satisfy even the heartiest eater.

2	heads romaine lettuce
2	medium tomatoes, chopped
4	ounces provolone cheese, cubed
4	ounces salami, cubed
½	cup choppd pepperoncini peppers
2	tablespoons capers, drained
2	tablespoons extra virgin olive oil
2	teaspoons red wine vinegar
	Pinch salt and freshly ground black pepper to taste

1. Remove the outer leaves from the heads of lettuce. Chop inner leaves. In a large bowl, place the chopped lettuce and remaining ingredients; toss to combine. Taste and adjust the seasonings, if necessary.

makes 4 servings

VENIERO'S
MANHATTAN, NYC

The East Village neighborhood has seen a lot of changes over the years. These days you'll see artsy fashion types and yuppies on its sidewalks, but step into Veniero's and you step back a century, into a mirror-lined cafe with pressed tin ceilings and marble floors.

Established in 1894 by Antonio Veniero, this bakery is still family owned. The 40-foot glass display case is full of pastries that most bakeries have stopped making because they're just too time-consuming (like the almond torte, a multilayered Sicilian confection that, to us, looked a little like a Vidalia onion). The baker who makes this fantasy of cookie crust, sponge cake, apricot jam, rum syrup, and marzipan took us back to the oldest bakery kitchen we've ever seen.

We rolled out the cookie bases on a 110-year-old table, then baked them in old rotating ovens (which sound like someone screaming as they turn) to give the pans even heat. Like any classic New York institution, the place is crammed so tight we could barely turn around, but that doesn't stop the guys at Veniero's from turning out cake after cake. We tried our hand at slicing the dome-shape sponge and brushing it with good, strong rum syrup, and whew! We were reeling. Sweet and intense, assembled with a baked coating of marzipan brushed with apricot glaze, that torte just cries out for a shot of espresso. It's no wonder Veniero's is still going strong—a slice of that cake and a cup of its coffee would keep anyone going 110 years!

Cinnamon Affogato

While we were at Veniero's, we learned about another Italian treat called affogato, which means "drowned." You pour hot espresso over ice cream that's been drizzled with caramelized sugar.

¼   cup sugar
¼   cup water
1   cinnamon stick
1   pint (2 cups) vanilla ice cream
1½   cups hot, strong-brewed coffee

1. In a small saucepan, combine sugar, water, and the cinnamon stick. Simmer over medium-high heat about 5 minutes, stirring until the sugar completely dissolves. Let syrup cool. Discard the cinnamon stick.

2. Scoop ice cream into 4 large coffee cups. Drizzle cinnamon syrup over ice cream. Pour hot coffee over ice cream. Serve immediately.

makes 4 servings

"This decadent dessert is dangerously easy to make." — BOBBY

Strawberry Cannoli Parfaits

As soon as we got home from New York, we put together what we learned at Veniero's and developed this recipe. There's no cannoli shell to fry, so it comes together quickly.

1 pound strawberries, hulled and sliced

3 tablespoons amaretto or orange liqueur

²/₃ cup heavy cream

¹/₃ cup confectioners' (powdered) sugar

1 cup ricotta cheese

¹/₂ teaspoon ground cinnamon

¹/₄ cup miniature semisweet chocolate chips

¹/₄ cup unsalted pistachios, chopped (optional)

24 amaretti cookies, crushed Miniature semisweet chocolate chips (optional)

1. In a medium bowl, combine the strawberries and amaretto. Cover and refrigerate at least 3 hours or overnight.

2. In a large bowl, whip the cream with the confectioners' sugar until soft peaks form (tips curl). In a medium bowl, stir half of the whipped cream into the ricotta to lighten it. Gently fold in the remaining whipped cream and cinnamon. Fold the ¹/₄ cup chocolate chips and the pistachios into cream mixture.

3. Place a layer of crushed amaretti cookies in each of 4 parfait glasses. Top each with a layer of cannoli cream and then strawberry slices. Repeat layering. If desired, top with additional miniature chocolate chips.

makes 4 servings

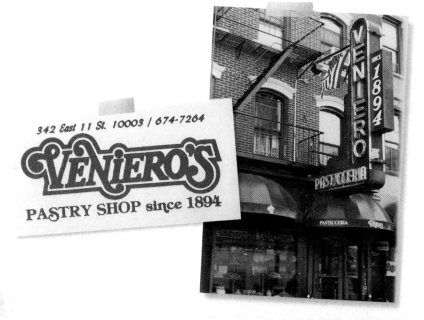

342 East 11 St. 10003 / 674-7264

VENIERO'S PASTRY SHOP since 1894

LANDI'S PORK STORE

BROOKLYN, NYC

Down South we're serious about pork, but Landi's may have us beat. We drove over the Brooklyn Bridge and deep into the "City of Kings" to get to this third-generation store. Painted on the front window is a giant pig wearing a crown, and inside is a family that specializes in anything and everything to do with pork. We thought we had found heaven when we walked in. Cured pork, fresh pork, sausage, salami—Landi's has it.

Landi's Pork Store has been in the same spot since 1958, and over the decades, it's offered olives, fresh pasta, homemade sauces, cheese, other meats, and home-cooked Italian specialties. Since the 1970s, the most popular product has been the rice balls. One look at those golden brown beauties and we knew they'd be out-of-this-world delicious!

The Landis made our day by giving us classic paper butcher caps to wear while we made the rice balls. We mixed cooked rice (15 pounds at a time) with an equal weight of fresh mozzarella and plenty of chopped pepperoni, salami, ham, and salty Pecorino Romano. We rolled this mixture into balls and dredged them in flour, beaten egg, and house-made bread crumbs, which have a healthy amount of cheese in them too. A dunk in the fryer leaves these snacks crisp on the outside, creamy in the middle, and absolutely addictive—even after making them for 40 years, the guys at Landi's can't get enough.

Sausage-Stuffed Pork Rolls

The recipe title pretty much says it all. This hot appetizer is our kind of ham and cheese!

6	4-ounce boneless, center-cut pork chops
12	ounces sweet or hot Italian sausage
3	ounces provolone cheese, cut into 6 narrow strips
6	fresh sage leaves
	Salt and freshly ground black pepper

1. With a mallet or heavy pan, pound each of the chops until very thin. Remove the casing from the sausage and crumble sausage into a skillet. Cook the sausage over medium heat about 10 minutes or until no trace of pink remains.

2. Preheat the broiler. Spoon about 2 tablespoons of the cooked sausage onto each pork chop. Top with one slice of provolone and one sage leaf. Roll each chop around filling and secure with a toothpick. Season the rolls with salt and pepper. Place pork rolls on a baking sheet or broiler pan.

3. Broil rolls 4 inches from heat for 5 to 6 minutes or until just done. Remove toothpicks before serving.

makes 4 to 6 servings

Almond-Stuffed Fried Olives

Over the years we've learned that just about everything tastes better if you fry it. This flavor-packed, breaded Italian snack is proof.

24	pitted green olives
24	smoked almonds
1/3	cup all-purpose flour
2	eggs, beaten
1/2	cup dried bread crumbs
	Peanut oil for frying

1. Pat the olives dry and stuff each with one almond, rounded end first. Roll olives in the flour, then dip into the beaten eggs, then roll in the bread crumbs.

2. In a heavy pot, heat 1 inch of peanut oil to 350°F. Fry the olives, in batches, about 20 to 30 seconds or until brown. Use a slotted spoon to remove olives from oil and drain on paper towels. Serve hot.

makes 4 to 6 servings

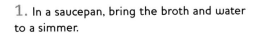

Risotto Cakes

If you like risotto as much as we do and you end up with leftovers, you can make these crispy fritters with risotto straight from the fridge. That's how the recipe was invented in the first place.

4	cups low-sodium chicken broth
1	cup water
2	tablespoons olive oil plus additional for sauteing
1	tablespoon unsalted butter
1	small yellow onion, chopped
1½	cups uncooked Arborio rice
½	cup white wine
1	cup frozen peas, thawed
1½	cups freshly grated Parmesan cheese
	Salt and freshly ground black pepper
1	cup dried bread crumbs

1. In a saucepan, bring the broth and water to a simmer.

2. Meanwhile, in a medium saucepan or large skillet, heat 2 tablespoons oil and the butter over medium heat. Add the onion; saute for 3 to 5 minutes or until translucent, stirring occasionally. Add rice; cook and stir for 1 minute, coating all the grains. Add the wine; cook and stir until it is almost evaporated. Add the simmering broth, ½ cup at a time; stir often and let almost all the liquid absorb before adding the next ½ cup. Continue adding broth in this way for 18 to 20 minutes or until the rice is creamy yet firm. (If you run out of broth before the rice is done, you can add simmering water.) Stir in the peas and Parmesan cheese; season to taste with salt and pepper. Let risotto cool.*

3. Form ¼-cup portions of the risotto into cakes. Dredge the cakes in the bread crumbs. In a large nonstick skillet, heat a thin film of additional oil over medium heat until shimmering. Saute the cakes, in batches, in the hot oil about 1 minute per side or until brown. Add more oil to skillet between batches as necessary. Serve hot.

 *You can refrigerate the risotto for up to one day at this point.

makes 20 cakes

ANIC "OSTRICH" SCRAMBLE
OBSTER
OMATO
AVIAR
REME FRAÎCHE

EIRLOOM TOMATO SOUP
REME FRAÎCHE
BASIL

2

ILLED PACIFIC ESCOLAR
ILTED RAPINI
UKON POTATO
HAMPAGNE BEURRE BLANC

M ALMOND FIG TART
ANDIED ORANGE
RT REDUCTION
ONEY ICE CREAM

COURSES

AMUSE

CHICKEN DUMPLING
morracan glaze

FIRST COURSE

HEIRLOOM TOMATO SALAD
gazpacho sorbet and baby purple basil

SECOND COURSE

GINGERED BEET FLAN
buttered lobster

THIRD COURSE

PAN SEARED DAY BOAT SCALLOP
cauliflower puree and sea urchin

FOURTH COURSE

SALT ROASTED NEW YORK STEAK
creamed chanterelles and veal cheek
sticks

FIFTH COURSE

SELECTION OF DESSERT
and petit fours

$ 85 per person

Gourmet Pops

Foie Gras Lollipops

Smoked Salmon Lollipop

Huckleberry Jam

DAVID BURKE & DONATELLA
MANHATTAN, NYC

It takes a great dad to come up with something his kids will eat when it's raining outside and there's only cream cheese and smoked salmon in the fridge—that's how Chef David Burke invented salmon pops. And it takes one of New York's quirkiest, most inventive celebrity chefs to realize the potential in those fun little foods-on-a-stick and to serve them on elegant lollipop "trees" at his glamorous Upper East Side restaurant.

We met with Richard Bies, David's pastry chef, who makes thousands of those famous pops every year in a whole range of flavors, from salmon to goat cheese to the most popular pop of all, cheesecake. We had to ask: How do you turn a cheesecake into a lollipop? Very simply: Take half a cheesecake (what you do with the other half is between you and your conscience) and whip it in a mixer. Pipe cheesecake blobs on a pan, put a stick in each one, chill until firm, and voilà! A cheesecake pop. Why didn't we think of that?

The fancy part comes with the toppings. Richard dips the pops in melted chocolate, crushed nuts, and even candy to make a good thing that much better. Fun, cute, familiar yet different, and easy to eat—we couldn't stop popping them!

Honey-Nut Goat Cheese Balls >

We like to serve this snack with wine or beer before a meal. They're a little sweet, a little salty, and a lot addictive!

4	ounces medium-firm fresh goat cheese
½	cup honey-roasted peanuts, finely chopped
	Honey for drizzling
	Freshly ground black pepper

1. Using a melon baller, scoop out rounds of goat cheese and form into balls with your hands.

2. Roll the balls in the chopped peanuts until completely covered. Drizzle balls lightly with honey and sprinkle with a little pepper. Serve with toothpicks.

makes about 16 balls

Cheesecake Surprise Balls

We used frozen cheesecake to create our own easy-to-make version of David Burke's cheesecake pops—with a surprise in the center.

1	18-ounce frozen cheesecake, thawed
36	fresh raspberries
1½	cups miniature semisweet chocolate chips

1. Scoop out 1 heaping teaspoon from the cheesecake. Use your hands to mold the cheesecake around a raspberry and roll the covered berry into a ball. Repeat with the remaining berries.

2. Roll the balls in the chocolate chips. Chill before serving.

makes about 36 pieces

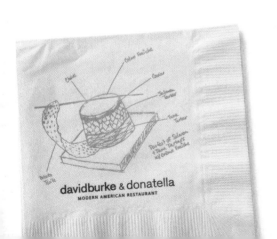

davidburke & donatella
MODERN AMERICAN RESTAURANT

ARTOPOLIS
QUEENS, NYC

How do you open a beautiful Greek bakery in Astoria, Queens? First take three Greek foodies who want to open a place that showcases their heritage. Then build a bakery—in Greece!—and have it shipped over in two huge containers. Finally add authentic home-style recipes for Greek breads, cakes, and pastries. The result: Artopolis.

Co-owner Regina Katopodis shared one of the bakery's Greek specialties, the galatoboureko (a Greek custard pastry). Regina talked us through the recipe, telling us how to stir together eggs, sugar, milk, and a little semolina for the filling. Did we mention stirring? Regina is as tough as Mama in the kitchen; if we stopped whisking for even a moment we were scolded.

To assemble the dessert we brushed layer after layer of paper-thin phyllo with clarified butter, then poured in the custard and topped it with more phyllo. The dessert takes on a rich color in the oven, and it gets a dousing with honey syrup as soon as it comes out. The result is creamy, flaky, crackly, sweet, and golden brown. The only thing that would have improved the experience would have been a little less hard work! We decided to stick to making Greek foods like salads and wraps at home. We're happy to leave the authentic desserts to the experts.

Greek Dolma Salad

Dolma are stuffed grape leaves filled with rice and seasonings that you can buy at Mediterranean specialty markets in the deli section. They're so hearty and tasty, they can turn a light Greek salad into a substantial meal.

2½	tablespoons olive oil
1	tablespoon freshly squeezed lemon juice
1	teaspoon chopped fresh oregano or thyme leaves
	Salt and freshly ground black pepper
1½	pounds cherry tomatoes, halved
1	large cucumber, peeled, seeded, and coarsely chopped
4	ounces feta cheese, crumbled
16	pitted Kalamata olives
8	ounces stuffed grape leaves, halved crosswise

1. In a small bowl, whisk together the oil, lemon juice, oregano, and salt and pepper to taste.

2. In a large bowl, combine the remaining ingredients except the stuffed grape leaves. Pour the vinaigrette over the salad, turning gently to coat. Arrange salad on serving plates and top evenly with stuffed grape leaves.

makes 4 servings

"Tangy and filling, this is my kind of salad." — BOBBY

Marinated Chicken Gyro Wraps

We developed our sandwich-making skills back in the Bag Lady days with Mama. This is one of our more recent favorites.

CHICKEN:

1½	pounds chicken cutlets, cut into 1-inch-long fingers
2	tablespoons olive oil
1	clove garlic, minced
1	teaspoon dried oregano
¾	teaspoon ground cumin
	Salt and freshly ground black pepper

YOGURT-DILL SAUCE:

1	cup Greek yogurt or plain yogurt
¼	cup finely chopped red onion
1	to 2 cloves garlic, minced
1½	tablespoons chopped fresh dill
2	teaspoons freshly squeezed lemon juice
	Salt and freshly ground black pepper

4	pita wraps, warm
1	cup shredded lettuce
1	cup chopped tomato
½	cup sliced cucumber

1. In a large bowl, place the chicken, oil, 1 clove garlic, oregano, cumin, and salt and pepper to taste; toss to coat. Cover with plastic wrap and refrigerate for 1 hour.

2. In a small bowl, stir together the Yogurt-Dill Sauce ingredients. Chill until ready to use.

3. Preheat the broiler. Spread the chicken on a baking sheet. Broil 6 inches from heat about 8 minutes or until cooked through.

4. To serve, spread each pita with some of the Yogurt-Dill Sauce. Divide the chicken, lettuce, tomato, and cucumber evenly among the pitas. If desired, top with additional sauce.

makes 4 servings

"The spice is right in these flavor-packed wraps." — BOBBY

ZOZO'S
MANHATTAN, NYC

Chefs Steve and Kyria Zobel have spent a lot of time in Brazil, and they took their experiences home to New York to open Zozo's, a Brazilian-style "fresh food diner." They filled the menu with fresh, healthy snacks and sandwiches, salads, juices, and fruit sorbets and shakes; then Kyria added some killer ice cream and amazing doughnuts to make up for the healthier stuff. You can guess what page of the menu we flipped right to.

Kyria makes the ice cream herself and puts some big flavors in her gelato-style creations. We loved the comforting combos she's dreamed up, such as peanut butter and marshmallow crème, and our favorite, the outrageously good mint gelato with chunks of chocolaty brownie. It was so good, we practically licked our bowls clean.

Kyria also cleared up a great frozen dessert mystery: the difference between ice cream and gelato. Kyria explained that while ice cream in America is usually made with equal parts milk and cream and only a little egg, European-style gelato uses a lower proportion of cream and more eggs, so it's a little lighter and more refreshing.

At Zozo's the gelato gets a wake-up call from peppermint. Then, when it's freshly churned and soft, Kyria folds in rich, fudgy pieces of her homemade brownies for an all-American flavor of Italian gelato, served in a Brazil-inspired diner on the Lower East Side. Only in New York!

Easy Biscuit Doughnuts

After eating homemade doughnuts with Kyria's gelato at Zozo's, we came home with a hankering for more—so we fried up some doughnuts like Mama always made, using biscuit dough to speed things along.

½ cup sugar
1 teaspoon ground cinnamon
Vegetable oil, for frying
1 12-ounce tube buttermilk
biscuit dough

1. In a small bowl, combine sugar and cinnamon. Set aside.

2. Fill a wide, shallow pan with 1 inch of oil. Heat the oil to 370°F.

3. Meanwhile, arrange the biscuits on a baking sheet. Using a 1-inch-diameter round cookie cutter, cut out the center of each biscuit. (Save the scraps to make bite-size doughnut holes.)

4. Drop the doughnuts into the hot oil and cook for 1 to 2 minutes or until golden brown, turning doughnuts if necessary. Transfer the doughnuts immediately to a baking sheet lined with paper towels and sprinkle generously with cinnamon sugar. Serve warm.

makes 10 doughnuts

"The only thing better than a homemade doughnut is two homemade doughnuts." —JAMIE

< Piña Colada Smoothies

Cool, fruity smoothies are terrific for breakfast drinking, and we blend them up all the time. This one is pretty good with a splash of rum in it too, if you're making a batch later in the day.

1	cup fresh pineapple chunks
1	cup unsweetened coconut milk
1	banana
¼	cup ice cubes
2	teaspoons honey (optional)
	Pineapple wedges for garnish

1. In a blender, combine the pineapple chunks, coconut milk, banana, ice, and, if desired, honey. Puree until smooth. Pour into 2 large glasses. Garnish each serving with a pineapple wedge.

makes 2 servings

Brûléed Banana Split

If you put a banana split in front of us, we turn right back into kids. We came up with this grown-up-sounding treat to give us an excuse to regress!

1	banana, peeled and split lengthwise
1	tablespoon packed dark brown sugar
1	scoop vanilla ice cream
1	scoop chocolate ice cream
1	scoop strawberry ice cream
	Chocolate sauce
	Caramel sauce
	Whipped cream
	Maraschino cherries

1. Preheat broiler. Line a rimmed baking sheet with foil. Lay the banana halves, cut sides down, on the baking sheet. Sprinkle each half with 1½ teaspoons of the brown sugar. Broil 4 to 5 inches from the heat about 2 minutes or until the sugar melts and starts to bubble. (Watch closely to make sure they don't burn.)

2. Place the scoops of ice cream in a bowl (a long banana-split bowl if you have one) and place the banana halves on either side. Top with chocolate and caramel sauces to taste, then the whipped cream and as many cherries as you can handle!

makes 1 banana split

MORRISON'S MAINE COURSE

PORTLAND, MAINE

The Morrison family has been lobstering and making lobster stew for more than a century, so when Don Morrison took us out on the wharf by his chowder house and set up the 100-year-old cast-iron kettle his grandfather used to use, we knew we were in the hands of a master. Surrounded by seagulls, boats, and fresh sea air, helping Don crack and pick lobsters, we began to get very hungry. But Don doesn't just steam his lobster, dunk it in butter, and call it dinner.

First he very gently sautes the lobster in butter with Maine sea salt and some paprika, which gives the stew a rich red color. Then Don adds the Maine chowder trinity: milk, cream, and evaporated milk. A pinch of sugar brings out the lobster's own sweetness, and the stew is cooked just until it steams—never boiled—to maximize the rich, delicate flavor.

While we were waiting for the stew, we traded lobster facts. We learned that one in every 33 million lobsters is blue and that lobster has less fat than chicken or fish (until the melted butter, that is!). Don said his lobster stew is so popular that he goes through 1,500 pounds of lobsters per week. When we finally sat down to a bowl, we were hungrier than a pair of lobstermen. It was worth the wait. Creamy, rich, delicate, sweet, and full of big, fresh lobster flavor and nothing more, that stew was like Maine in a bowl.

Lobster Rolls

Unless you're on the Maine coast, you're better off making lobster rolls than buying them. You can also serve the lobster salad in avocado halves.

4	1½-pound cooked lobsters or 4 lobster tails or 1½ pounds lobster meat
½	cup mayonnaise
3	tablespoons freshly squeezed lemon juice
2	inner celery stalks and leaves, finely chopped
2	tablespoons chopped fresh parsley leaves
	Freshly ground black pepper
4	rolls, split and lightly toasted
	Melted butter for brushing

1. Remove the meat from the lobsters, chopping any large chunks into bite-size pieces. In a bowl, combine the lobster meat, mayonnaise, lemon juice, celery, parsley, and pepper to taste.

2. Brush cut sides of the rolls with melted butter and fill with the lobster salad.

makes 4 servings

Creamy Clam and Corn Chowder

5	slices bacon, coarsely chopped
2	tablespoons unsalted butter
1	large onion, finely chopped
2	medium red bliss or russet potatoes, peeled and finely chopped
2	celery stalks, finely chopped
1	teaspoon dried thyme
3	cups low-sodium chicken broth
	Salt and freshly ground black pepper
2½	cups half-and-half
2	6½-ounce cans chopped clams in clam juice, undrained
3	cups frozen corn kernels, thawed
	Chopped fresh Italian parsley leaves
	Bottled hot pepper sauce (optional)

1. In a large saucepan, cook bacon over medium-low heat for 10 to 15 minutes or until crisp, stirring occasionally. Add butter and stir to combine. Add onion, potatoes, celery, and thyme. Increase heat to medium and saute about 10 minutes or until onion softens. Add the broth; bring to a boil. Reduce heat and simmer about 10 minutes or until potatoes are tender. Season to taste with salt and pepper.

2. Stir in the half-and-half, clams, and corn. Reduce heat to low. Cover and cook for 20 minutes. Taste and adjust the seasoning, if necessary. Ladle the chowder into bowls and garnish with chopped parsley. If desired, serve with hot sauce.

makes 6 servings

Chunky Shrimp Bisque

Although we had never eaten lobster stew before our trip to Maine, we've always loved Mama's wonderful shrimp bisque.

6	tablespoons unsalted butter
1	large onion, finely chopped
2	small cloves garlic, minced
1	bay leaf
1	teaspoon dried thyme
3	tablespoons all-purpose flour
6	cups low-sodium chicken broth
2	cups canned chopped tomatoes, drained
1	cup heavy cream
2	tablespoons dry sherry
2	pounds medium shrimp, peeled, deveined, and coarsely chopped
	Salt and freshly ground black pepper
	Chopped fresh Italian parsley leaves (optional)
	Oyster crackers (optional)

1. In a Dutch oven or large saucepan, melt butter over medium heat. Add the onion, garlic, bay leaf, and thyme. Cook about 10 minutes or until the onion is tender, stirring frequently. Add flour; cook and stir for 2 minutes. Add broth, whisking until well combined. Add tomatoes; bring to a boil. Reduce heat and simmer, partially covered, for 30 minutes.

2. Add cream and sherry; simmer for 10 minutes. Add shrimp; cook about 2 minutes or until shrimp turn pink and are cooked through. Season to taste with salt and pepper.

3. Remove the bay leaf and puree half of the soup in a blender. Return the pureed soup to the pot and stir to combine. (Or use an immersion blender to puree the soup until it reaches a chunky, half-pureed consistency.) Heat through. Ladle the bisque into bowls and, if desired, garnish with chopped parsley and oyster crackers.

makes 6 servings

EMINGER BERRIES
AUBURN, MAINE

It took a guy to look at a strawberry and say, "Hey, wouldn't this be better if it were stuffed with a dessert like cheesecake, crème brûlée, tiramisu, pecan pie, or cookie dough and then dipped in chocolate?" It took chef Susan Eminger, that guy's wife, to figure out how to do it. And it took great big, red, flavor-packed premium Maine strawberries to make it all possible.

For her cheesecake version, Susan starts by making a nice dense New York-style cheesecake with plenty of cream cheese and a graham cracker crust. Then she does the kind of thing that we might have gotten hollered at for doing when we were kids: She grabs the whole cheesecake with both hands and mashes it all up until the crust and filling are combined.

Susan slices each strawberry up to the stem and pats as much cheesecake mixture in and around the berry as she possibly can—about a whole slice worth. Then she wishes the berry good luck, takes hold of the stem, and very gently dips the whole thing in chocolate. She decorates it with white chocolate and graham cracker crumbs, then chills it to set the chocolate.

The finished dessert looks spiffier than berries, chocolate, and cake combined and tastes even better than that. The smooth, creamy tang of the cheesecake and the juicy taste of the berry strike such a perfect balance with the chocolate covering that we left wondering why we ever ate cheesecake the regular way. You learn something every day—life is sweet that way.

Luscious Chocolate Cheesecake

Tasting the cheesecake-stuffed berries at Eminger's, we were reminded that there are few better combos. We went right home and made up a chocolate cheesecake that's just perfect with strawberries on top.

CRUST:

1	9-ounce box chocolate wafer cookies
6	tablespoons unsalted butter, melted

FILLING:

1½	cups heavy cream
1	tablespoon unsweetened cocoa powder
1	11½-ounce bag bittersweet chocolate chips
2	8-ounce packages cream cheese, softened
¾	cup sugar
1	tablespoon cornstarch
1	cup sour cream
2	teaspoons vanilla
3	large eggs

GLAZE:

¼	cup heavy cream
2	ounces bittersweet chocolate, chopped
1	quart strawberries, hulled

1. Preheat oven to 350°F. For the crust, grease a 9-inch springform pan and wrap the outside with a double layer of foil. In a food processor, finely grind the cookies. Add the melted butter and process until blended. Press the mixture into the bottom and partly up the sides of the pan. Place pan in the refrigerator.

2. For the filling, in a saucepan, combine 1½ cups cream and the cocoa. Cook and stir over medium heat until the cocoa dissolves. Reduce heat and whisk in chocolate chips until smooth. Set aside and let cool.

3. In a large bowl, beat together the cream cheese and sugar until smooth. Beat in the cornstarch. Beat in the sour cream and vanilla. Add the eggs, one at a time, beating after each addition. Fold 1 cup of the cream cheese mixture into the chocolate mixture to lighten it, then scrape the chocolate mixture into the cream cheese mixture. Whisk until smooth.

4. Pour the filling into the springform pan. Place the springform pan inside a large baking pan. Fill the baking pan with 1 inch of hot water. Bake the cake about 1 hour or until just set and slightly puffed. Let cake cool in the baking pan on a wire rack. Cover the cake with plastic wrap and chill overnight.

5. For the glaze, in a small saucepan, bring ¼ cup cream to a boil. Reduce the heat and whisk in the chopped chocolate until combined. Let cool. Use a knife to loosen the cake from the pan, then remove the sides of the pan. Arrange the strawberries on top of the cake and drizzle with the glaze.

makes 10 to 12 servings

Cream Cheese-and-Pecan-Stuffed Berries

These romantic, elegant-looking treats are simple to make.
Serve them as part of a dessert buffet or even at a fancy brunch.

32	whole large strawberries, hulled
12	ounces cream cheese, softened
½	cup confectioners' (powdered) sugar
¼	teaspoon vanilla or almond extract
⅔	cup chopped pecans

1. Cut a thin slice from the bottom of each strawberry so the berries stand upright. Place berries, cut sides down, on a serving platter. Carefully cut the berries into 4 wedges, cutting almost to, but not through, the bottoms. Fan wedges just slightly, taking care not to break them. Set aside.

2. In a mixing bowl, beat together the cream cheese, sugar, and vanilla until combined but still stiff. Using a teaspoon or pastry bag with decorative tip, fill the strawberries with the cream cheese mixture. Sprinkle chopped pecans on top of the stuffed strawberries. Cover and refrigerate until ready to serve.

makes about 32 pieces

"berries made better"— BOBBY

WICKED WHOOPIES
GARDINER, MAINE

Amy Bouchard's success story is a lot like Mama's, except that while Mama was going door to door with her Bag Lady lunches, Amy was making whoopie. Whoopie pies are Amy's specialty, a recipe of her grandma's that she makes with an especially light touch. She makes the pies by sandwiching round pillows of rich chocolate cake with sweet and fluffy marshmallow crème filling. When Amy's brother suggested that she start selling the pies, she thought he was crazy, but she gave it a shot.

The first year Amy went door to door, carrying her baby girl in one arm and a basket of whoopie pies in the other. Over time, her home business picked up until it outgrew her home. Now she has made over a million dollars, and her bakery turns out 7,000 whoopie pies every day!

The recipe is the same as always, and Amy's husband, brother, mother-in-law, son, and daughter all pitch in, so the whoopie pies are still as homey, sweet, and lovingly made as ever. Amy makes 20 different pies, including maple, strawberry, pumpkin, and chocolate chip, and she uses different flavors of filling. She also guarantees that there are 10 smiles in every whoopie pie.

We had to agree that those pies were wicked good, as Mainers like to say. Then Amy presented us with her jumbo five-pound whoopie pie. We figured there were about 100 smiles in that pie—it was almost big enough to share!

Lattice-Top Blueberry Pie

Maine is justly famous for its tiny wild blueberries, which bake up into a spectacular pie. Serve this with a scoop of ice cream for a taste of summer à la mode!

1	15-ounce package rolled refrigerated unbaked piecrusts (2 crusts)
3	pints blueberries, rinsed and dried
¾	cup sugar
⅓	cup quick-cooking tapioca
2	teaspoons finely grated lemon zest
1	tablespoon freshly squeezed lemon juice
¼	teaspoon ground cinnamon

1. Preheat oven to 400°F. Let piecrusts stand at room temperature for 15 minutes or as directed on package. Meanwhile, in a large bowl, toss together the blueberries, sugar, tapioca, lemon zest, lemon juice, and cinnamon. Set aside.

2. Line a 9-inch pie plate with 1 of the piecrusts. Using a sharp knife, slice the remaining piecrust into ½-inch-wide strips.

3. Spoon the blueberry mixture into the pie shell. Arrange the piecrust strips in a lattice pattern on top. Flute edges of crust. Place the pie on a foil-lined rimmed baking sheet.

4. Bake for 30 minutes. Reduce oven temperature to 350°F. Bake for 20 to 25 minutes more or until the berries are bubbling and the crust is golden. Transfer pie to a rack to cool before serving.

makes 8 servings

Mini Whoopie Pies

There's only one reason to make whoopie pies miniature—so you can eat more of them. We love to take these cream-filled, cakey sandwiches along on picnics.

CHOCOLATE CAKES:

2¼	cups all-purpose flour
½	cup unsweetened cocoa powder
1	teaspoon baking soda
2	teaspoons cream of tartar
1	teaspoon salt
⅔	cup vegetable shortening
1¼	cups granulated sugar
2	large eggs
2	teaspoons vanilla
1	cup milk

FILLING:

½	cup (1 stick) unsalted butter, softened
1	cup confectioners' (powdered) sugar
2	cups marshmallow crème
1	teaspoon vanilla

1. Preheat oven to 350°F. Grease 2 large baking sheets; set aside.

2. In a bowl, whisk together the flour, cocoa, baking soda, cream of tartar, and salt; set aside. In the bowl of an electric mixer, cream together the shortening and granulated sugar. Beat in the eggs and the 2 teaspoons vanilla. Alternately add the flour mixture and milk, beating until fully combined.

3. Drop dough by tablespoons 2 inches apart onto prepared baking sheets. Bake for 8 to 10 minutes or until darker around the edges and firm to the touch. Transfer cakes to a wire rack to cool completely.

4. For the filling, beat together the butter and confectioners' sugar. Beat in the marshmallow crème and the 1 teaspoon vanilla until smooth. Spoon about 1 tablespoon filling onto the bottom of a cake. Press the bottom of a second cake against filling to make a sandwich. Repeat with remaining cakes and filling. To store, layer whoopie pies between sheets of waxed paper in an airtight container and refrigerate for up to 2 days.

makes about 24 pies

MOM'S APPLE PIE COMPANY
LEESBURG, VIRGINIA

When we heard about a pie place called Mom's, we said, "These folks may have some pretty-looking pies, but they're not our mom's, so how good can they be?" We ate our words after we met Petra Cox, the cook and daughter in a pie-making, fruit-farming family that knows its way around a pie plate just about as well as our family does.

Petra was out in the fields when we drove up, and we helped her pick some of the biggest, ripest blackberries we have ever seen. The freshly picked fruit goes right into a pie without being precooked, and she doesn't add any more sugar than she needs to, so there's nothing between you and that fresh fruit taste when you cut into the crispy, golden crumb topping.

Nothing, that is, except plenty of real butter. Petra hand-rolls her all-butter crust for the bottom of the pie, fills it up to the brim with fruit, and then makes a pecan streusel blend to go on top. As it bakes, the pie smells like a blackberry field, and it looks amazing when it's done, with thick, purple fruit juices bubbling up from under that golden topping.

The berries in that pie were so good, and not too sweet, but what really made all the difference was that old-timey all-butter crust. It was so good we almost didn't need a scoop of vanilla ice cream on the side. Almost.

Three-Berry Corn Muffins

We love muffins for breakfast. In these, the warm, rich flavor of corn is a perfect base for sweet, juicy berries.

1	cup self-rising cornmeal mix
¾	cup all-purpose flour
2	tablespoons sugar
¼	teaspoon baking soda
⅛	teaspoon salt
1	cup sour cream
½	cup (1 stick) unsalted butter, melted
2	eggs
½	cup hulled and sliced strawberries
½	cup blackberries
½	cup blueberries

1. Preheat oven to 375°F. Grease a 12-cup muffin tin; set aside.

2. In a large bowl, whisk together the cornmeal mix, flour, sugar, baking soda, and salt. In a separate bowl, whisk together the sour cream, butter, and eggs. Stir the sour cream mixture into the cornmeal mixture until just combined. (Do not overmix.) Fold in the berries.

3. Divide the batter evenly among the prepared muffin cups. Bake for 20 to 25 minutes or until golden and a toothpick inserted in the center of a muffin comes out clean. Let cool in pan for 5 minutes before removing and serving.

makes 12 muffins

"I just love these tender, sunny treats." — PAULA

Blackberry and Peach Cobbler

Our family finds it hard to choose what to do with ripe summer fruit. Do we make a cobbler or a pie? Cobbler is a little easier, so here's the recipe for one of our favorites. Substitute any ripe fruit for the berries and peaches.

4	cups pitted and sliced peaches (about 2 pounds)
2	cups blackberries
½	cup granulated sugar
2	tablespoons cornstarch
1½	cups all-purpose flour
½	cup packed light brown sugar
2	teaspoons baking powder
½	teaspoon salt
6	tablespoons cold unsalted butter, cubed
¾	cup heavy cream
	Vanilla ice cream (optional)

1. Preheat oven to 350°F. Grease a 9-inch square baking pan or casserole dish; set aside.

2. In a bowl, toss together the peaches, blackberries, granulated sugar, and cornstarch; set aside. In a second bowl, whisk together the flour, brown sugar, baking powder, and salt. Cut in the butter until the mixture resembles coarse crumbs. Stir in the cream until just combined.

3. Spread the fruit mixture in the bottom of the prepared pan. Drop the biscuit batter by spoonfuls on top of the fruit. Bake for 45 to 55 minutes or until golden brown on top and bubbling. Let cool for 10 minutes before serving. If desired, serve with ice cream.

makes 6 servings

Filet Mignon with Blackberries

Tart blackberries are an unexpected complement to a great steak. We serve this recipe when we want to impress.

4	6-ounce filet mignon steaks (beef tenderloin)
	Salt and freshly ground black pepper
2	tablespoons olive oil
¼	cup finely chopped shallots
½	cup dry red wine, such as Cabernet Sauvignon
1	cup low-sodium beef broth
3	tablespoons blackberry preserves
2	tablespoon unsalted butter
	Fresh blackberries for garnish

1. Pat the steaks dry with a paper towel and season generously with salt and pepper. In a heavy skillet, heat the oil over medium-high heat until almost smoking. Sear the steaks in the hot oil for 3 minutes per side for medium rare. Transfer steaks to a serving plate, tent with foil, and let stand.

2. Using the same skillet, saute the shallots for 1 minute. Add the red wine, scraping up any browned bits on the bottom of the pan. Let wine boil until reduced by half. Add broth and blackberry preserves; return to a boil and reduce by half. (The sauce should coat the back of a spoon.) Whisk in the butter. Season sauce with additional salt and pepper to taste.

3. To serve, drizzle the sauce over the steaks and scatter a few blackberries on the plate.

makes 4 servings

MARKET INN RESTAURANT

WASHINGTON, D.C.

Washington, D.C., is crab country, just a quick scuttle from Chesapeake Bay. The family-owned Market Inn Restaurant has been making crab cakes from the same recipe since 1959 and serving them to diplomats, senators, and all the movers and shakers in town, so we knew where to go for our crab cake fix.

General manager Michael Kipp walked us through the restaurant and showed us the bell that was rung to call the senators back to Congress for a vote and the table where some heated conversations took place during Watergate. Then we headed into the kitchen to learn about the crab cakes that all these history-making politicians come back for year after year.

The cooks at the Market Inn have been there almost as long as the restaurant has

and since they make about 100,000 crab cakes a year, they know the subject inside and out. They make jumbo lump baked cakes and classic fried cakes. In both cases, the main ingredient is fresh, sweet lump crabmeat—plenty of it. The baked cakes are just mounds of big pieces of crabmeat, gently held together with mayonnaise, mustard, dried parsley, and cracker crumbs, then baked to a beautiful brown. The fried cakes have a mix of fresh carrot, onion, celery, parsley, oil, butter, and hot sauce that gives them a sweet and spicy flavor.

We did a taste test, alternately savoring the crispy, flavorful, golden brown patties and the succulent crab-packed lump cakes, and we concluded that this is a debate on which we cannot take sides. When it comes to crab cakes, we're nonpartisan.

Hot Crab Canapés

We knew this recipe was a winner the moment we brought the little crab-topped crackers out of the kitchen. They disappeared faster than kids shove off from the table when it's time to clear the plates.

8	ounces flake or lump crabmeat
½	cup shredded Swiss cheese
⅓	cup mayonnaise
2	tablespoons chopped black olives
1	tablespoon chopped red onion
1	tablespoon freshly squeezed lemon juice
1	teaspoon Dijon mustard
¼	teaspoon salt
	Freshly ground black pepper to taste
1	8-ounce box rich round crackers

1. Preheat the broiler. In a bowl, combine all of the ingredients except the crackers. Evenly spread 1 generous teaspoon of the crab mixture on a cracker, taking care to cover the whole cracker. Repeat with the remaining mixture.

2. Place the canapés on a baking sheet. Broil 6 inches from heat for 1 to 2 minutes or until hot and golden (watch carefully so they do not burn). Serve immediately.

makes about 42 pieces

"Holy crab, these sure are good!" — JAMIE

Crab-Corn Cakes with Basil-Jalapeño Sauce

We put our own spin on crab cakes by adding corn and plenty of flavorful ingredients, including scallions and mustard. Then we top the crispy cakes with a savory, herby tartar sauce.

CRAB CAKES:

3	tablespoons unsalted butter
4	scallions, trimmed and finely chopped
1	clove garlic, minced
1	pound crab claw meat
½	cup frozen corn, thawed
½	cup dried bread crumbs
1	egg
3	tablespoons mayonnaise
1	tablespoon Dijon mustard
2	teaspoons chopped fresh parsley leaves
	Freshly ground black pepper
2	tablespoons vegetable oil
⅓	cup yellow cornmeal

BASIL-JALAPEÑO TARTAR SAUCE:

½	cup mayonnaise
1	jalapeño, seeded and finely chopped
1	clove garlic, minced
2	tablespoons chopped fresh basil leaves
2	teaspoons capers, drained and chopped
1½	teaspoons freshly squeezed lemon juice
	Pinch salt
	Freshly ground black pepper

1. In a medium skillet, heat 1 tablespoon of the butter over medium-high heat. Add the scallions and garlic. Cook and stir for 2 to 3 minutes or until softened. Place the mixture in a large bowl. Add the crabmeat, corn, bread crumbs, egg, mayonnaise, mustard, parsley, and pepper to taste; mix well. Divide the mixture into 12 portions and form into ½-inch-thick patties. Place the patties on a baking sheet and chill for 1 hour.

2. Meanwhile, in a small bowl, stir together all of the tartar sauce ingredients. Refrigerate until ready to use.

3. Preheat oven to 375°F. In a large skillet, heat the remaining 2 tablespoons butter and the oil over medium-high heat. Dredge each crab cake in the cornmeal, turning to coat evenly. Sear the cakes for 3 to 4 minutes per side or until golden brown. Return the crab cakes to the baking sheet. Bake for 10 minutes. Serve crab cakes hot with Basil-Jalapeño Tartar Sauce.

makes 6 servings

Crab and Artichoke Quiche

We love crab, artichokes, and quiche, so it was only a matter of time until we combined the three. The result was so delicious, you might want to make a double recipe.

2	tablespoons unsalted butter
½	cup chopped onion
1	stalk celery, finely chopped
¾	cup marinated artichokes, rinsed, drained, and chopped
4	eggs
1	cup heavy cream
1	teaspoon bottled hot pepper sauce
1	teaspoon Worcestershire sauce
½	teaspoon salt
	Freshly ground black pepper
4	ounces cream cheese, cubed
1	9- to 10-inch prepared single piecrust, partially baked
¼	cup shredded Parmesan cheese
6	ounces flaked or lump crabmeat

1. Preheat oven to 350°F. In a medium skillet, melt the butter over medium heat. Add the onion and celery. Cook and stir about 5 minutes or until softened. Add the artichokes; cook for 1 minute more. Set aside. In a bowl, whisk together the eggs, cream, hot sauce, Worcestershire sauce, salt, and pepper to taste. Set aside.

2. Spread the cream cheese cubes evenly in the bottom of the piecrust. Sprinkle the Parmesan over the cream cheese. Spread the artichoke mixture and the crabmeat over the cheeses. Fill the crust with the egg mixture.

3. Bake for 35 to 40 minutes or until just set. Let stand for 5 minutes before serving.

makes 8 servings

STICKY FINGERS BAKERY

WASHINGTON, D.C.

We grew up on Mama's great home cooking, and we agree on most things when it comes to dinner. But dessert is another story. I [Jamie] have the family sweet tooth, while Bobby has healthier leanings. When we heard about a cinnamon bun that would make us both happy, we were skeptical. What could be healthy about a gooey cinnamon bun?

What couldn't? That's what two friends, Doron Greenblatt Petersan and Kirsten Rosenberg, asked when they decided to open a bakery that leaves out the dairy, eggs, and cholesterol in favor of healthier, vegan options. Right from the start they were determined not to leave out the sticky-sweet goodness, so they named their venture Sticky Fingers Bakery.

Sticky Fingers makes mouthwatering oatmeal-cream cookie sandwiches, chocolate cake, chocolate chip cookies, and the plumpest, softest, best-looking cinnamon swirls that any sweet tooth could hope for. How do they do it?

Doron and Kirsten took us behind the scenes so we could see how more healthful ingredients, including soymilk, organic flours, canola- and olive oil-based shortenings, and minimally refined sugar come together to make buns that are moist, sticky, light and soft, warm and creamy, and also low in saturated fat and cholesterol. With their healthier cinnamon swirls, these two friends have created gooey, sweet perfection that everyone will love.

Honey Snickerdoodles

Cinnamon and honey are a natural match. These chewy, crackle-topped cookies are perfect with a glass of sweet tea.

1¾	cups all-purpose flour
1½	teaspoons baking powder
1	teaspoon baking soda
⅛	teaspoon salt
¾	teaspoon ground cinnamon
½	cup (1 stick) unsalted butter
1	cup plus 3 tablespoons sugar
1	egg
1½	teaspoons honey
1¼	teaspoons vanilla

1. Preheat oven to 375°F. Grease 2 large baking sheets; set aside.

2. In a bowl, whisk together the flour, baking powder, baking soda, salt, and ¼ teaspoon of the cinnamon; set aside. In the bowl of an electric mixer, beat the butter and 1 cup of the sugar together until fluffy. Beat in the egg, honey, and vanilla. Slowly beat in the flour mixture.

3. In a small bowl, combine the remaining 3 tablespoons sugar and the remaining ½ teaspoon cinnamon. Form the dough into 1-inch balls. Roll the balls in the sugar-cinnamon mixture. Place the balls 2 inches apart on the prepared baking sheets.

4. Bake for 10 to 12 minutes or until golden brown and slightly cracked on the top. Transfer cookies to a wire rack to cool.

makes about 42 cookies

Spicy Cinnamon French Toast

We decided to take French toast to new places, and this is what we came up with. It's a recipe worth waking up for.

1	cup packed light brown sugar
½	cup (1 stick) unsalted butter, melted
1½	cups whole milk
2	eggs
1	teaspoon vanilla
1	teaspoon freshly squeezed lemon juice
¾	teaspoon ground cinnamon
	Pinch salt
	Pinch cayenne pepper
12	slices whole wheat, challah, or French bread

1. Preheat oven to 375°F. In a bowl, whisk together the sugar and melted butter. Spread the mixture in a large rimmed baking pan. Set aside.

2. In a large bowl, whisk together the milk, eggs, vanilla, lemon juice, cinnamon, salt, and cayenne pepper. Dip each slice of bread in the egg mixture and soak for 30 seconds. Transfer to the baking pan. Bake about 25 minutes or until golden, turning halfway through baking.

makes 6 servings

A

Affogato, Cinnamon, 163
Alaskan Salmon Salad with
    Iceberg Lettuce, 100, 101
Almonds
    Almond-Stuffed Fried Olives, 167
    Cinnamon Bear Cub Claws, 117
    Lemony Honey-Almond
        Tea Cakes, 30, 31
Appetizers
    Almond-Stuffed Fried Olives, 167
    Cheesy Pretzel Dipping
        Sauce, 130, 131
    Classic Cheese Fondue, 113
    Coconut Fried Shrimp, 20, 21
    Grape, Blue Cheese, and Walnut
        Bites, 80, 81
    Honey-Nut Goat Cheese
        Balls, 172, 173
    Hot Crab Canapés, 205
    Hummus with Pita
        and Vegetables, 76, 77
    Lime-Marinated Chicken Wings
        with Avocado Dip, 26, 27
    Pecan-Crusted Cranberry
        Cheese Balls, 113
    Prosciutto-Wrapped Cheese
        Straws, 144
    Salami, Mozzarella, and
        Basil-Tomato Skewers, 146, 147
Apples
    Apple-Bacon Corn Bread, 105
    Boy Scout Baked Apples, 150, 151
    Bratwurst and Granny
        Smith Apple Salad, 139
    Caramel Apple-Nut
        Crumb Pie, 152, 153
Avocado Dip, 26, 27

B

Bacon
    Apple-Bacon Corn Bread, 105
    Bacon-Wrapped Corn on the Cob, 58
Baked Mac and Cheese, 114, 115

Bananas
    Brûléed Banana Split, 185
    Chilly Banana Pudding, 102, 103
    Elvis' Favorite Tea Sandwich, 32, 33
    Piña Colada Smoothies, 184, 185
Bar cookies
    Espresso Brownies, 46, 47
    Tennessee Whiskey Fruit and Nut
        Bars, 36, 37
Basil-Jalapeño Tartar Sauce, 206
BBQ Chicken, The Deen
    Brothers', 40, 41
Beans
    Brat and Bean Casserole, 139
    Hummus with Pita
        and Vegetables, 76, 77
    White Bean Soup, 108, 109
Beef
    Filet Mignon with
        Blackberries, 202, 203
Beer Brats, Midwestern-Style, 140, 141
Berries
    Blackberry and Peach
        Cobbler, 200, 201
    Cheesecake Surprise Balls, 172
    Cream Cheese-and-Pecan-Stuffed
        Berries, 192, 193
    Filet Mignon with
        Blackberries, 202, 203
    Lattice-Top Blueberry Pie, 195
    Luscious Chocolate Cheesecake, 191
    Pecan-Crusted Cranberry
        Cheese Balls, 113
    Strawberry Cannoli Parfaits, 164, 165
    Three-Berry Corn Muffins, 199
Biscuit Doughnuts, Easy, 182, 183
Bisque, Chunky Shrimp, 188, 189
Blackberries
    Blackberry and Peach
        Cobbler, 200, 201
    Filet Mignon with
        Blackberries, 202, 203
Blueberries
    Lattice-Top Blueberry Pie, 195
    Three-Berry Corn Muffins, 199

Blue Cheese, Grape, and
    Walnut Bites, 80, 81
Boy Scout Baked Apples, 150, 151
Bratwurst
    Brat and Bean Casserole, 139
    Bratwurst and Granny
        Smith Apple Salad, 139
    Midwestern-Style
        Beer Brats, 140, 141
Breads
    Apple-Bacon Corn Bread, 105
    Spicy Cinnamon French
        Toast, 212, 213
    Three-Berry Corn Muffins, 199
Brownie Cakes with Rose
    Whipped Cream, 45
Brownies, Espresso, 46, 47
Brown Sugar Divinity, 85
Brûléed Banana Split, 185

C

Cabbage
    Easy Coleslaw, 96, 97
Cakes
    Brownie Cakes with Rose
        Whipped Cream, 45
    Cherry-Stuffed Pecan Streusel
        Coffee Cake, 106, 107
    Double-Chocolate Icebox Cake, 103
    Lemony Honey-Almond
        Tea Cakes, 30, 31
    Luscious Chocolate Cheesecake, 191
    Southern-Style Coconut Cake, 18, 19
    Upside-Down Pear Gingerbread, 77
Canapés, Hot Crab, 205
Candy
    Brown Sugar Divinity, 85
    Chocolate and Caramel
        Turtles, 86, 87
    The William Truffles, 69
Cannoli Parfaits, Strawberry, 164, 165
Caramel Apple-Nut
    Crumb Pie, 152, 153

Food photographs are noted in colored numerals.

Casseroles
Baked Mac and Cheese, 114, 115
Brat and Bean Casserole, 139
Corn Bread Casserole with
Pickled Jalapeños, 42, 43
Creamed Corn and Fried
Onion Casserole, 51
Cheese
Baked Mac and Cheese, 114, 115
Cheesecake Surprise Balls, 172
Cheesy Pretzel Dipping
Sauce, 130, 131
Chopped Salad, Arthur-Avenue
Style, 161
Classic Cheese Fondue, 113
Cream Cheese-and-Pecan-Stuffed
Berries, 192, 193
The Deen Brothers' Deep-Dish
Pizza, 126, 127
Goat Cheese Grits, 64, 65
Grape, Blue Cheese, and
Walnut Bites, 80, 81
Greek Dolma Salad, 176, 177
Honey-Nut Goat
Cheese Balls, 172, 173
Hot Crab Canapés, 205
Luscious Chocolate Cheesecake, 191
Pecan-Crusted Cranberry
Cheese Balls, 113
Prosciutto-Wrapped
Cheese Straws, 144
Ratatouille Supreme with
Pepper Jack, 66, 67
Risotto Cakes, 168, 169
Salami, Mozzarella, and Basil-Tomato
Skewers, 146, 147
Sausage-Stuffed Pork Rolls, 167
Southern-Stuffed Loaf, 158, 159
Strawberry Cannoli Parfaits, 164, 165
Cheesecake, Luscious Chocolate, 191
Cheesecake Surprise Balls, 172
Cheese Straws, Prosciutto-
Wrapped, 144
Cherry-Stuffed Pecan Streusel
Coffee Cake, 106, 107

Chicken
The Deen Brothers' BBQ
Chicken, 40, 41
Lime-Marinated Chicken Wings
with Avocado Dip, 26, 27
Marinated Chicken Gyro
Wraps, 178, 179
Roasted Lemon Chicken
with Red Grapes, 82, 83
Chickpeas
Hummus with Pita and
Vegetables, 76, 77
Chiles
Basil-Jalapeño Tartar Sauce, 206
Chipotle Collard Greens, 43
Corn Bread Casserole with
Pickled Jalapeños, 42, 43
Chilly Banana Pudding, 102, 103
Chipotle Collard Greens, 43
Chocolate
Brownie Cakes with Rose
Whipped Cream, 45
Cheesecake Surprise Balls, 172
Chocolate and Caramel
Turtles, 86, 87
Chocolate Chip Pie, 52, 53
Chocolate-Peanut Butter
Chippers, 134, 135
Double-Chocolate Icebox Cake, 103
Espresso Brownies, 46, 47
Goldbrick Sundaes, 126
Luscious Chocolate Cheesecake, 191
Mini Whoopie Pies, 196, 197
Tennessee Whiskey Fruit
and Nut Bars, 36, 37
Truffle Pie, 70, 71
Vanilla Chocolate Chip Root Beer
Floats, 122, 123
The William Truffles, 69
Chopped Salad, Arthur
Avenue-Style, 161
Chowder, Creamy Clam and Corn, 187
Chunky Shrimp Bisque, 188, 189
Cinnamon Affogato, 163
Cinnamon Bear Cub Claws, 117
Cioppino, The Deen Brothers', 90, 91

Clams
Creamy Clam and Corn Chowder, 187
The Deen Brothers' Cioppino, 90, 91
Classic Cheese Fondue, 113
Cobbler, Blackberry and
Peach, 200, 201
Coconut
Coconut-Fried Shrimp, 20, 21
Mango Coconut Rice, 14, 15
Piña Colada Smoothies, 184, 185
Southern-Style Coconut Cake, 18, 19
Coffee
Cinnamon Affogato, 163
Espresso Brownies, 46, 47
Coffee Cake, Cherry-Stuffed Pecan
Streusel, 106, 107
Collard Greens, Chipotle, 43
Cookies and bars
Chocolate–Peanut Butter
Chippers, 134, 135
Delicate Danish Butter
Cookies, 118, 119
Espresso Brownies, 46, 47
Honey Snickerdoodles, 211
Many Jam Thumbprints, 136, 137
Tennessee Whiskey Fruit
and Nut Bars, 36, 37
Corn
Bacon-Wrapped Corn on the Cob, 58
Corn Bread Casserole with Pickled
Jalapeños, 42, 43
Crab-Corn Cakes with Basil-Jalapeño
Sauce, 206, 207
Creamed Corn and Fried Onion
Casserole, 51
Creamy Clam and Corn Chowder, 187
Low-Country Boil, 94, 95
Corn Bread, Apple-Bacon, 105
Corn Bread Casserole with
Pickled Jalapeños, 42, 43
Cornmeal
Apple-Bacon Corn Bread, 105
Three-Berry Corn Muffins, 199
Crabmeat
Crab and Artichoke
Quiche, 208, 209

Crab-Corn Cakes with
    Basil-Jalapeño Sauce, 206, 207
The Deen Brothers' Cioppino, 90, 91
Hot Crab Canapés, 205
Cranberry Cheese Balls,
    Pecan-Crusted, 113
Cream cheese
    Crab and Artichoke
        Quiche, 208, 209
    Cream Cheese-and-Pecan-
        Stuffed Berries, 192, 193
    Luscious Chocolate Cheesecake, 191
Creamed Corn and Fried
    Onion Casserole, 51
Creamy Clam and Corn Chowder, 187
Custard Pie, Two-Grape, 80

D

The Deen Brothers' BBQ
    Chicken, 40, 41
The Deen Brothers' Cioppino, 90, 91
The Deen Brothers' Deep-
    Dish Pizza, 126, 127
Delicate Danish Butter Cookies, 118, 119
Desserts
    Blackberry and Peach
        Cobbler, 200, 201
    Boy Scout Baked Apples, 150, 151
    Brownie Cakes with Rose
        Whipped Cream, 45
    Brown Sugar Divinity, 85
    Brûléed Banana Split, 185
    Caramel Apple-Nut
        Crumb Pie, 152, 153
    Cheesecake Surprise Balls, 172
    Cherry-Stuffed Pecan Streusel
        Coffee Cake, 106, 107
    Chilly Banana Pudding, 102, 103
    Chocolate and Caramel
        Turtles, 86, 87
    Chocolate Chip Pie, 52, 53
    Chocolate-Peanut Butter
        Chippers, 134, 135
    Cinnamon Affogato, 163
    Cinnamon Bear Cub Claws, 117

Cream Cheese-and-Pecan-Stuffed
    Berries, 192, 193
Delicate Danish Butter
    Cookies, 118, 119
Double-Chocolate Icebox Cake, 103
Easy Biscuit Doughnuts, 182, 183
Espresso Brownies, 46, 47
Goldbrick Sundaes, 126
Honey Snickerdoodles, 211
Key Lime Pie with Meringue
    Topping, 24, 25
Kringle Bread Pudding, 119
Lattice-Top Blueberry Pie, 195
Lemony Honey-Almond
    Tea Cakes, 30, 31
Luscious Chocolate Cheesecake, 191
Many Jam Thumbprints, 136, 137
Mini Whoopie Pies, 196, 197
Southern-Style Coconut Cake, 18, 19
Strawberry Cannoli Parfaits, 164, 165
Tennessee Whiskey Fruit and Nut
    Bars, 36, 37
Truffle Pie, 70, 71
Two-Grape Custard Pie, 80
Upside-Down Pear Gingerbread, 77
Vanilla Chocolate Chip Root Beer
    Floats, 122, 123
The William Truffles, 69
Dips
    Avocado Dip, 26, 27
    Cheesy Pretzel Dipping
        Sauce, 130, 131
    Classic Cheese Fondue, 113
    Dipping Sauce, 20, 21
    Hummus with Pita
        and Vegetables, 76, 77
Divinity, Brown Sugar, 85
Dolma Salad, Greek, 176, 177
Double-Chocolate Icebox Cake, 103
Doughnuts, Easy Biscuit, 182, 183
Drinks
    Mint Juleps, 35
    Piña Colada Smoothies, 184, 185
    Texas Margaritas, 58, 59

Vanilla Chocolate Chip Root Beer
    Floats, 122, 123
Dry-Rub Baby Back Ribs, 56, 57

E

Easy Biscuit Doughnuts, 182, 183
Easy Coleslaw, 96, 97
Eggplant
    Ratatouille Supreme with Pepper
        Jack, 66, 67
Elvis' Favorite Tea Sandwich, 32, 33
Espresso Brownies, 46, 47

F

Fajitas, Fish, 74, 75
Feta cheese
    Greek Dolma Salad, 176, 177
Filet Mignon with
    Blackberries, 202, 203
Fish
    Alaskan Salmon Salad with Iceberg
        Lettuce, 100, 101
    The Deen Brothers' Cioppino, 90, 91
    Fish Fajitas, 74, 75
    Fried Halibut Sandwiches, 96, 97
    Grilled Salmon with Key Lime
        Butter, 27
    Zesty Grilled Grouper, 14, 15
Fondue, Classic Cheese, 113
French Toast, Spicy Cinnamon, 212, 213
Fried Halibut Sandwiches, 96, 97
Frosting, 7-Minute, 18, 19
Fruit. See also specific fruits
    Tennessee Whiskey Fruit and
        Nut Bars, 36, 37

G

Ginger Ale-Glazed Ham, 122
Gingerbread, Upside-Down Pear, 77
Goat cheese
    Goat Cheese Grits, 64, 65
    Honey-Nut Goat Cheese
        Balls, 172, 173
Goldbrick Sundaes, 126

Grapes
  Grape, Blue Cheese, and Walnut
    Bites, 80, 81
  Roasted Lemon Chicken
    with Red Grapes, 82, 83
  Two-Grape Custard Pie, 80
Greek Dolma Salad, 176, 177
Greens
  Alaskan Salmon Salad with Iceberg
    Lettuce, 100, 101
  Chipotle Collard Greens, 43
  Chopped Salad, Arthur
    Avenue-Style, 161
  Sauteed Spinach with Sweet
    Vidalia Onion, 13
Grilled Rosemary Lamb Chops, 64, 65
Grilled Salmon with Key Lime
  Butter, 27
Grits, Goat Cheese, 64, 65
Grouper, Zesty Grilled, 14, 15
Gumbo, Shrimp, 89

H

Halibut, Fried, Sandwiches, 96, 97
Ham
  Ginger Ale-Glazed Ham, 122
  Prosciutto, Carpaccio-Style, 160, 161
  Prosciutto and Melon Salad, 144, 145
  Prosciutto-Wrapped Cheese
    Straws, 144
Honey-Nut Goat Cheese Balls, 172, 173
Honey Snickerdoodles, 211
Hot Crab Canapés, 205
Hummus with Pita and
  Vegetables, 76, 77

I

Ice cream
  Brûléed Banana Split, 185
  Cinnamon Affogato, 163
  Goldbrick Sundaes, 126
  Vanilla Chocolate Chip Root Beer
    Float, 122, 123

K

Key Lime Pie with Meringue
  Topping, 24, 25
Kringle Bread Pudding, 119

L

Lamb Chops, Rosemary, 64, 65
Lattice-Top Blueberry Pie, 195
Lemony Honey-Almond
  Tea Cakes, 30, 31
Lettuce
  Alaskan Salmon Salad with Iceberg
    Lettuce, 100, 101
  Chopped Salad, Arthur Avenue-
    Style, 161
Limes
  Key Lime Pie with Meringue
    Topping, 24, 25
  Lime-Marinated Chicken Wings
    with Avocado Dip, 26, 27
  Texas Margaritas, 58, 59
Lobster Rolls, 187
Low-Country Boil, 94, 95
Luscious Chocolate Cheesecake, 191

M

Mac and Cheese, Baked, 114, 115
Main dishes
  Alaskan Salmon Salad with Iceberg
    Lettuce, 100, 101
  Baked Mac and Cheese, 114, 115
  Brat and Bean Casserole, 139
  Bratwurst and Granny Smith
    Apple Salad, 139
  Crab and Artichoke
    Quiche, 208, 209
  Crab-Corn Cakes with Basil-Jalapeño
    Sauce, 206, 207
  The Deen Brothers' BBQ
    Chicken, 40, 41
  The Deen Brothers' Cioppino, 90, 91
  The Deen Brothers' Deep-Dish
    Pizza, 126, 127
  Dry-Rub Baby Back Ribs, 56, 57

Filet Mignon with
  Blackberries, 202, 203
Fish Fajitas, 74, 75
Ginger Ale-Glazed Ham, 122
Grilled Rosemary Lamb Chops, 64, 65
Grilled Salmon with Key Lime
  Butter, 27
Lime-Marinated Chicken Wings with
  Avocado Dip, 26, 27
Low-Country Boil, 94, 95
Midwestern-Style Beer
  Brats, 140, 141
Roasted Lemon Chicken with Red
  Grapes, 82, 83
Sausage-Stuffed Pork Rolls, 167
Shrimp Gumbo, 89
Whiskey-Glazed Pork Loin, 35
Zesty Grilled Grouper, 14, 15
Mango Coconut Rice, 14, 15
Many Jam Thumbprints, 136, 137
Margaritas, Texas, 58, 59
Marinated Chicken Gyro
  Wraps, 178, 179
Melon and Prosciutto Salad, 144, 145
Midwestern-Style Beer Brats, 140, 141
Mini Whoopie Pies, 196, 197
Mint Juleps, 35
Muffins, Three-Berry Corn, 199

N

Nuts. *See also Pecans*
  Almond-Stuffed Fried Olives, 167
  Brown Sugar Divinity, 85
  Caramel Apple-Nut
    Crumb Pie, 152, 153
  Chocolate and Caramel
    Turtles, 86, 87
  Chocolate-Peanut Butter
    Chippers, 134, 135
  Cinnamon Bear Cub Claws, 117
  Grape, Blue Cheese, and
    Walnut Bites, 80, 81
  Honey-Nut Goat Cheese
    Balls, 172, 173

Lemony Honey-Almond
Tea Cakes, 30, 31
Tennessee Whiskey Fruit and Nut
Bars, 36, 37

O

Olives
Almond-Stuffed Fried Olives, 167
Greek Dolma Salad, 176, 177
Onions
Creamed Corn and Fried Onion
Casserole, 51
Sauteed Spinach with Sweet
Vidalia Onion, 13

P

Pasta
Baked Mac and Cheese, 114, 115
Peach and Blackberry
Cobbler, 200, 201
Peanut butter
Chocolate-Peanut Butter
Chippers, 134, 135
Elvis' Favorite Tea Sandwich, 32, 33
Peanuts
Chocolate-Peanut Butter
Chippers, 134, 135
Honey-Nut Goat Cheese
Balls, 172, 173
Pear Gingerbread, Upside-Down, 77
Peas
Risotto Cakes, 168, 169
Pecans
Caramel Apple-Nut
Crumb Pie, 152, 153
Cherry-Stuffed Pecan Streusel
Coffee Cake, 106, 107
Chocolate and Caramel
Turtles, 86, 87
Cream Cheese-and-Pecan-Stuffed
Berries, 192, 193
Goldbrick Sundaes, 126
Many Jam Thumbprints, 136, 137
Pecan-Crusted Cranberry
Cheese Balls, 113

Tennessee Whiskey Fruit and Nut
Bars, 36, 37
The William Truffles, 69
Pepper Jack, Ratatouille
Supreme with, 66, 67
Peppers. See also Chiles
Chopped Salad, Arthur Avenue-
Style, 161
Midwestern-Style Beer
Brats, 140, 141
Southern Stuffed Loaf, 158, 159
Pies
Caramel Apple-Nut
Crumb Pie, 152, 153
Chocolate Chip Pie, 52, 53
Key Lime Pie with Meringue
Topping, 24, 25
Lattice-Top Blueberry Pie, 195
Mini Whoopie Pies, 196, 197
Truffle Pie, 70, 71
Two-Grape Custard Pie, 80
Piña Colada Smoothies, 184, 185
Pizza, Deep-Dish, The
Deen Brothers', 126, 127
Pork. See also Bacon;
Ham; Sausages
Dry-Rub Baby Back Ribs, 56, 57
Sausage-Stuffed Pork Rolls, 167
Whiskey-Glazed Pork Loin, 35
Potatoes
Low-Country Boil, 94, 95
Pretzel Dipping Sauce,
Cheesy, 130, 131
Prosciutto
Prosciutto, Carpaccio-Style, 160, 161
Prosciutto and Melon Salad, 144, 145
Prosciutto-Wrapped Cheese
Straws, 144

Q

Quiche, Crab and Artichoke, 208, 209

R

Raisins
Cinnamon Bear Cub Claws, 117
Kringle Bread Pudding, 119

Ratatouille Supreme with
Pepper Jack, 66, 67
Rice
Mango Coconut Rice, 14, 15
Risotto Cakes, 168, 169
Risotto Cakes, 168, 169
Roasted Lemon Chicken with
Red Grapes, 82, 83
Root Beer Floats, Vanilla
Chocolate Chip, 122, 123

Rose Whipped Cream, 45
Russian Dressing, 100, 101

S

Salads
Alaskan Salmon Salad with Iceberg
Lettuce, 100, 101
Bratwurst and Granny Smith Apple
Salad, 139
Chopped Salad, Arthur
Avenue-Style, 161
Easy Coleslaw, 96, 97
Greek Dolma Salad, 176, 177
Prosciutto, Carpaccio-Style, 160, 161
Prosciutto and Melon Salad, 144, 145
Salami
Chopped Salad, Arthur Avenue-
Style, 161
Salami, Mozzarella, and Basil-Tomato
Skewers, 146, 147
Salmon
Alaskan Salmon Salad with Iceberg
Lettuce, 100, 101
Grilled Salmon with Key Lime
Butter, 27
Sandwiches
Elvis' Favorite Tea Sandwich, 32, 33
Fried Halibut Sandwiches, 96, 97
Lobster Rolls, 187
Marinated Chicken Gyro
Wraps, 178, 179
Shrimp Salad Sandwiches, 50, 51
Southern Stuffed Loaf, 158, 159
Turkey and Cranberry Mayo
Pretzel Sandwiches, 131

Sauces
Basil-Jalapeño Tartar Sauce, 206
Dipping Sauce, 20, 21
Yogurt-Dill Sauce, 179
Sausages
Brat and Bean Casserole, 139
Bratwurst and Granny Smith
Apple Salad, 139
Chopped Salad, Arthur
Avenue-Style, 161
Low-Country Boil, 94, 95
Midwestern-Style Beer
Brats, 140, 141
Salami, Mozzarella, and Basil-Tomato
Skewers, 146, 147
Sausage-Stuffed Pork Rolls, 167
Shrimp Gumbo, 89
Sauteed Spinach with Sweet Vidalia
Onion, 13
Shellfish
Chunky Shrimp Bisque, 188, 189
Coconut Fried Shrimp, 20, 21
Crab and Artichoke
Quiche, 208, 209
Crab-Corn Cakes with Basil-Jalapeño
Sauce, 206, 207
Creamy Clam and Corn Chowder, 187
The Deen Brothers' Cioppino, 90, 91
Hot Crab Canapés, 205
Lobster Rolls, 187
Low-Country Boil, 94, 95
Shrimp Gumbo, 89
Shrimp Salad Sandwiches, 50, 51
Side dishes
Apple-Bacon Corn Bread, 105
Bacon-Wrapped Corn on the Cob, 58
Baked Mac and Cheese, 114, 115
Boy Scout Baked Apples, 150, 151
Chipotle Collard Greens, 43
Corn Bread Casserole with Pickled
Jalapeños, 42, 43
Creamed Corn and Fried Onion
Casserole, 51
Easy Coleslaw, 96, 97
Goat Cheese Grits, 64, 65

Mango Coconut Rice, 14, 15
Ratatouille Supreme with
Pepper Jack, 66, 67
Risotto Cakes, 168, 169
Sauteed Spinach with Sweet Vidalia
Onion, 13
Smoothies, Piña Colada, 184, 185
Snickerdoodles, Honey, 211
Soups & Stews
Chunky Shrimp Bisque, 188, 189
Creamy Clam and Corn Chowder, 187
The Deen Brothers' Cioppino, 90, 91
Shrimp Gumbo, 89
White Bean Soup, 108, 109
Southern Stuffed Loaf, 158, 159
Southern-Style Coconut Cake, 18, 19
Spicy Cinnamon French Toast, 212, 213
Spinach, Sauteed, with Sweet Vidalia
Onion, 13
Squash
Ratatouille Supreme with Pepper
Jack, 66, 67
Strawberries
Cream Cheese-and-Pecan-Stuffed
Berries, 192, 193
Luscious Chocolate Cheesecake, 191
Strawberry Cannoli Parfaits, 164, 165
Three-Berry Corn Muffins, 199
Sundaes, Goldbrick, 126

T
Tartar Sauce, Basil-Jalapeño, 206
Tennessee Whiskey Fruit and Nut
Bars, 36, 37
Texas Margaritas, 58, 59
Three-Berry Corn Muffins, 199
Tomatoes
Chopped Salad, Arthur-Avenue
Style, 161
Greek Dolma Salad, 176, 177
Prosciutto, Carpaccio Style, 160, 161
Ratatouille Supreme with
Pepper Jack, 66, 67
Salami, Mozzarella, and Basil-Tomato
Skewers, 146, 147

Truffle Pie, 70, 71
Truffles, The William, 69
Turkey and Cranberry Mayo Pretzel
Sandwiches, 131
Turtles, Chocolate and Caramel, 86, 87
Two-Grape Custard Pie, 80

U
Upside-Down Pear Gingerbread, 77

V
Vanilla Chocolate Chip Root Beer
Floats, 122, 123
Vegetables. See also
specific vegetables
Hummus with Pita and
Vegetables, 76, 77

W
Walnuts
Brown Sugar Divinity, 85
Caramel Apple-Nut
Crumb Pie, 152, 153
Grape, Blue Cheese, and Walnut
Bites, 80, 81
Whipped Cream, Rose, 45
Whiskey
Mint Juleps, 35
Tennessee Whiskey Fruit and Nut
Bars, 36, 37
Whiskey-Glazed Pork Loin, 35
White Bean Soup, 108, 109
Whoopie Pies, Mini, 196, 197
The William Truffles, 69

Y
Yogurt-Dill Sauce, 179

Z
Zesty Grilled Grouper, 14, 15
Zucchini
Ratatouille Supreme with
Pepper Jack, 66, 67

SPECIAL THANKS

Just like a favorite recipe that needs every ingredient to make it just right, this book could not have happened without every person below who made it possible.

Thanks to Mom and Dad for making us who we are. We love y'all. Thanks to Brooke who, while pregnant with sore feet and all, helped with scheduling and kept us cruising on the road. Thanks to Aunt Peggy and Uncle Bubba for all the support.

To Melissa Clark for all the heavy lifting.

To our Lady & Sons team. Without y'all, we couldn't have hit the road. Dustin Walls, the big man, our GM—you're just like our brother; Scott Hopke, our kitchen manager: We are so thankful and proud of you. And our entire management team: Rance Jackson, Dora Charles, Cookie Espinoza, Karl Schumacher, Brandon Jones, Jeff Cooler, Darell Myers, Ashley Kelly, Erik Lindsey, Daniel Porter, Kent Eastman, Adam Nations, Buffy Nelson, Andrew Lee, Emily Schmidt, John Gallien, Melvin Thomas, Shane Roberts, Jay Hiers, and Teresa Luckey.

Thank you to Gordon Elliott and Mark Schneider with Follow Productions who made us and our show look great. And to our *Road Tasted* travel crew: Sweets, Winks, Juggs, Buttons, The Hammer, DH, Crash, The Rock, Ro, Heath, and Danille. "Here's to everything."

Thank you to the Meredith Books creative team who made our dream come true. Jan, Lois, Mick, and Erin, you are awesome.

And thank you to our agent, Barry Weiner, and literary agent, Janis Donnaud, who really made it all possible.

A special thanks to the Food Network for giving us our chance. We hope we made you proud.

Last, thank you to all the folks that invited *Road Tasted* into your homes and businesses. Small business is the true backbone of America and your hard work and spirit are the true story of our entire project.

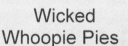

Alaska Silk Pie Co.
3429 Airport Way S
Seattle, WA 98134
800/745-5743
alaskasilkpie.com

Artopolis Bakery
Patisserie
Agora Plaza
23-18 31st St.
Astoria, NY 11105
800/553-2270
artopolis.net

Beechwood Cheese Co.
N1598W County Rd. A
Beechwood, WI 53001
877/224-3373
beechwoodcheese.com

Bendtsen's Bakery, Inc.
3200 Washington Ave.
Racine, WI 53405
262/633-0365
bendtsensbakery.com

Blond Giraffe
107 Simonton St.
Key West, FL 33040
888/432-6283
blondgiraffe.com

Butters Brownies
800/975-6309
buttersbrownies.com

Conch Republic
Seafood Company
631 Greene St.
Key West, FL 33040
305/294-4403
conchrepublicseafood.com

David Burke & Donatella
133 E. 61st St.
New York, NY 10021
212/813-2121
gourmetpops.com
dbdrestaurant.com

Eminger Berries
9 Grove St.
Auburn, ME 04210
888/642-3779
emingerberries.com

Flagstaff House
Restaurant
1138 Flagstaff Rd.
Boulder, CO 80302
303/442-4640
flagstaffhouse.com

Kim & Scott's
Gourmet Pretzels
2107 W. Carroll Ave.
Chicago, IL 60612
800/578-9478
kimandscotts.com

Landi's Pork Store
5909 Avenue N.
Brooklyn, NY 11234
718/763-3230
brooklynporkstore.com

Lou Malnati's Pizzeria
6649 N. Lincoln Ave.
Lincolnwood, IL 60712
847/673-0800
loumalnatis.com

Lynchburg Cake
& Candy Co.
134 Cashion Rd.
Lynchburg, TN 37352
931/759-7179
lynchburgcakeandcandy.com

Macrina Bakery and Cafe
2408 1st Ave.
Seattle, WA 98121
206/448-4032
macrinabakery.com

Marini's Candies
2608 Mission St.
Santa Cruz, CA 95060
866/627-4647
mariniscandies.com

Market Inn Restaurant
200 E St. SW
Washington, DC 20024
202/554-2100
marketinnrestaurant.com

Mike's Deli
2344 Arthur Ave.
Bronx, NY 10458
866/272-5264
arthuravenue.com

Mom's Apple Pie Co.
220 Loudoun St. SE
Leesburg, VA 20176
703/ 771-8590
momsapplepieco.com

Morrison's Maine Course
Maine Wharf
72 Commercial St.
Portland, ME 04101
877/783-9496
morrisonsmaine.com

Neely's Bar-B-Que
Restaurant
670 Jefferson Ave.
Memphis, TN 38103
901/521-9798
neelysbbq.com

Phil's Fish Market
& Eatery
7600 Sandholtd Rd.
Moss Landing, CA 95039
831/633-2152
philsfishmarket.com

Pike Place Fish Market
86 Pike Place
Seattle, WA 98101
800/542-7732
pikeplacefish.com

Royers Round Top Cafe
105 Main St.
Round Top, TX 78954
877/866-7437
royersroundtopcafe.com

Solomon's Gourmet
Cookies
2222 N. Elston Ave.
Chicago, IL 60614
888/384-8575
solomonscookies.com

Sprecher Brewing Co.
701 W. Glendale Ave.
Glendale, WI 53209
414/964-2739
sprecherbrewery.com

Sticky Fingers Bakery
1370 Park Rd. NW
Washington, DC 20010
202/299-9700
stickyfingersbakery.com

Sweetie Pies
520 Main St.
Napa, CA 94559
707/257-8817
sweetiepies.com

Swiss Meat & Sausage Co.
2056 S. Hwy. 19
Hermann, MO 65041
800/793-7947
swissmeats.com

Tennessee T-Cakes, Inc.
200 Hill Ave. Suite 3
Nashville, TN 37210
888/886-3926
tntcakes.com

The Art of Baking
by Henrietta
316 Petronia St.
Key West, FL 33040
305/295-0505
henriettakeywest.com

The Blue Owl
Restaurant and Bakery
6116 2nd St.
Kimmswick, MO 63053
636/464-3128
theblueowl.com

The Boulder
Dushanbe Teahouse
1770 13th St.
Boulder, CO 80302
303/442-4993
boulderteahouse.com

The County Line
6500 W. Bee Cave Rd.
Austin, TX 78746
512/327-1742
countyline.com

Veniero's
342 East 11th St.
New York, NY 10003
212/674-7070
venierospastry.com

Volpi Italian Foods
5250 Daggett Ave.
St. Louis, MO 63110
800/288-3439
volpifoods.com

Wen Chocolates
720/891-4622
wenchocolates.com

Wicked Whoopies
5 Mechanic St.
Gardiner, ME 04345
877/447-2629
wickedwhoopies.com

Zozo's
172 Orchard St.
New York, NY 10002
212/228-0009
zozosnyc.com